ISBN 978-1-334-04561-5
PIBN 10598094

1 MONTH OF
FREE
READING

at

www.ForgottenBooks.com

By purchasing this book you are eligible for one month membership to ForgottenBooks.com, giving you unlimited access to our entire collection of over 1,000,000 titles via our web site and mobile apps.

To claim your free month visit:

www.forgottenbooks.com/free598094

The
ART OF WRITING
OPERA-LIBRETTOS

Practical Suggestions

By

EDGAR ISTEL

Translated
From the German Manuscript by
Dr. TH. BAKER

G. SCHIRMER, INC.
New York

PREFACE

There are many composers in the world who think it strange that their operas have so little success, although they are recognized as excellent musicians. The idea may gradually dawn upon these good fellows, but bad dramatists, that the cause of their ill success is to be sought simply in the fact that they know nothing about the stage or the planning of a libretto. But how shall they learn to do better?

Hitherto there has been no book that gave really practical directions for the planning and analytical criticism of an opera-libretto. Shortly before the war I published a work which might be considered as the first attempt at writing such a book. The abundant experience which the author has had since then as a poet and composer in producing and staging several of his own operas, has encouraged him (on request of Mr. O. G. Sonneck) to rewrite the aforesaid work in a form specially adapted for American conditions. In doing so, all theoretical discussions of a general character have been reduced to the narrowest limits, so that the practical part could be proportionately enlarged. I trust that the young American writer may learn from the example of the best among the vigorous European operatic works of all the nations considered, that the principal thing is the action and its development, and that everything must be avoided which is not genuinely theatrical. Then—I do not doubt —original modern American operas will soon be produced and take their place in the world-repertory beside the masterworks of a Bizet, a Verdi, and a Wagner.

EDGAR ISTEL.

BERLIN, Summer of 1920.

CONTENTS

[v]

Contents

[vi]

CHAPTER I

COMPOSER AND LIBRETTIST

To the modern music-dramatist various possibilities are open with regard to the attitude he may assume toward the libretto problem.

1. Gluck's Procedure

A dramatically skilled and musical poet inspires the composer, who, as he himself asserts, strives while composing to forget that he is a musician. "However talented a composer may be, he will always write only mediocre music if the poet does not arouse in him that enthusiasm without which the works of all the arts are weak and flabby," wrote the master to the editor of the "Mercure de France." Gluck's dictum applies to all composers of true dramatic feeling, but musically immature. He remarks succinctly, that one can always write effective music to good librettos, but only impotent music to a poor book. Although the opera-books of Gluck, in their original shape (Wagner, as we know, effectively remodeled the "Iphigenia in Aulis"), scarcely answer the demands of modern dramatic technics in their construction and characterization, his adherence to the above

[1]

principle, taking into account his peculiar individuality, nevertheless raised Gluck to a commanding position in the history of opera. And even to-day a composer of dramatic emotionality, though less gifted musically, might have the better chance to win operatic success with a libretto based on an intimate knowledge of stage-effect—always providing that the poet has given due heed to the specifically musical requirements. To be sure, as really good librettos are remarkably scarce, this case will not occur with alarming frequency. As a modern instance we might mention the book, very skillfully adapted by R. Lothar from a Spanish (Catalonian) drama by Guimera, of d'Albert's "Tiefland." However, the composers of such books stand or fall according to the effectiveness of their librettos—a fact vividly illustrated by the changeful stage-fortunes of d'Albert.

2. Mozart's Procedure

In contrast to Gluck, who waits upon the Word, the master of "Figaro" and "Don Giovanni" takes his departure from Music. "In an opera the poem must unquestionably be the obedient daughter of the music," he writes in a letter of Oct. 13, 1781, to his father. This phrase characterizes the Italian conception as opposed to the more French view of Gluck. Such an exuberant musical invention of so inexhaustible power, as only Wolfgang Amadeus Mozart possessed, might in its full consciousness of genius feel assured, even when subjecting the poet to its will, that it would hit the true mean of musical expression and, however luxuriant the musical investiture, never lose sight of the close-knit dramatic construction. True, it was only in Da Ponte that Mozart found a congenial librettist, who understood how to adapt himself to the master while providing him with books nicely calculated for stage-effect. It makes little difference that Da Ponte was no original genius; he was a skillful adapter, who furnished precisely what Mozart needed, and without him we should have been the poorer by two immortal masterworks. So it came, that Mozart could confidently assert: "The best plan, then, is for a good composer, who understands the stage and can himself take a certain initiative, to combine with a clever poet as a veritable phœnix."—Note these words, "as a veritable phœnix"! There can be no doubt concerning the rarity of this happy combination. Rossini's books for the "Barber of Seville" (by E. Sterbini) and "Tell" (by Étienne and Bis), Verdi's best librettos ("Rigoletto," "La Traviata" and "Amelia," by Piave, "Aida" by Ghislanzoni, "Otello" and "Falstaff" by Boito), Bizet's "Carmen," by Meilhac and Halévy, show such favorable coincidences. Verdi had, besides, the peculiar good fortune, in the case of his last two master-works, "Otello" and "Falstaff," to find in Boito a librettist who was himself an opera composer and therefore well aware of what had to be done. More recently Puccini has taken the lead in securing the effective, albeit very gross, librettos to "Tosca" and "Butterfly" from Illica and Giacosa. Among French librettists must be mentioned Carré and Barbier, who cleverly adapted "Marguerite" (Faust) for Gounod, "Mignon" for Thomas, and "The Tales of Hoffmann" for Offenbach. In Germany, the country poorest in theatrical talent, we may name W. Friedrich (*recte* Riese), a theatre poet well instructed in French methods, who helped Flotow to win his only permanent successes ("Martha," "Stradella"); also Mosenthal, librettist of Nicolai's "Merry Wives of Windsor." Above all, however, it is the much-abused Scribe, one of the most admirable librettists of all times and peoples, who stands well-nigh un-rivalled in his knowledge of stagecraft and of the requirements of music. This is proved by numerous opera-books of his that are still in vogue, and are constructed with a truly genial discernment for stage-effect. Among the most striking examples are four books written for Auber: "Le Part du Diable," "Le Domino noir," "Fra Diavolo," and "La Muette de Portici." Another masterpiece is the text to "La Juive," for Halévy. In between, Scribe admittedly wrote inferior librettos as well, which is not a matter for surprise, considering his wholesale production. He came into ill repute chiefly through his librettos for Meyerbeer: "Robert le Diable," "Les Huguenots," "Le Prophète," "L'Africaine," but this was only because he sometimes allowed himself to be bullied by the composer, who was always aiming at writing effective musical numbers, into departing from his well-established dramatic principles. After all, for Meyerbeer these were the best operabooks imaginable, and no small measure of credit is due to Scribe that the above works obtained worldwide success. And in fine, whatever one may please to think about the partnership of Meyerbeer and Scribe, the best work of the twain, "Les Huguenots," will still live on the stage when a thousand operatic weaklings of a later date have long been consigned to oblivion.

3. Lortzing's Procedure

This is a purely empirico-practical fabrication of opera-texts for one's own use, emanating *in toto* from the requirement for animated theatrical effect. How Lortzing tackled this problem is very clearly described by himself in a conversation published by J. C. Lobe in "Konsonanzen und Dissonanzen" (Leipzig, 1869), a work now almost forgotten. Below I quote the most important points:

LOBE:—Our conversation turned to opera-texts, and I asked him why he adapted existing pieces for his operas, instead of inventing something of his own.

LORTZING:—I tried that at first with a few short pieces, but it requires more talent than I possess, and longer study and practice than were at my disposal! I soon came to the conclusion that many more enjoyable things would be proffered us in the world of art if every talent sought to perfect itself within the bounds set for it by nature, without reaching out after fruits which are beyond its grasp. So I was glad to turn my attention to unremembered plays and adapt them for my use as operas. The actor has one advantage which most dramatic poets lack— familiarity with the stage. After one has been playing his tricks before the public almost daily for some twenty years, he gradually learns from his audiences what makes a hit and what does not. How delightfully many a tirade, many a jest, reads in a book, and how perfectly flat it falls on the stage. Contrariwise, much that looks like nothing at all in print strikes fire from the soul when acted to the life. And so one finally comes to realize the significance of the *placing* of dialogues and scenes. Therefore, every dramatic poet ought really to be an actor for a time.

Having my knowledge of the stage, I might well venture on the adaptation of good plays. And yet—how long did I have to seek for a suitable subject! When I thought I had at last found such an one, I first of all asked myself whether it contained musical situations, scenes capable of stirring the emotions. These scenes I marked, to begin with. Here was an opportunity for a song, there for an aria, elsewhere for a duet, an ensemble, a chorus, etc. When I found these in a piece, a weight was lifted from my heart. Next began another task—that of a critic, so to speak. I asked, What are the most effective scenes in it? which are weaker ones, or quite unfit? Then the weak scenes had to be improved; the unfit ones were discarded. Little by little my plan took on the form that I needed for an opera, and with that the most formidable difficulties were vanquished. The dialogue was easily altered, and the verse—well, my goodness, who is there nowadays that can't patch together some sort of verses, let alone opera-verses! Why overexert oneself? For everything that goes to make up poetry—profound, majestic thoughts, rosy imagery, purity of rime, smoothness and flow of language, and all the rest, must be burned to ashes by the composer in order that the phœnix of music may arise therefrom. Rôles!—that is the "open sesame" to the doors of the stage alike for the dramatic poet and the composer. There are singers with little voice, who still are pretty good actors, and other singers who sing well but act poorly. Now, if one has found a piece which provides the former with good acting parts, and the latter with nice singing parts, a favorable reception is assured. Most success is had with such rôles as cannot be "knocked out" even by the small fry among the histrionic tribe—rôles that play themselves, like those of the Burghermaster and Peter the Great in "Tsar and Carpenter." Mind you, those are what I call rôles, and the Italians understand that kind best of all, which accounts for their success. The singers are always attracted by pieces that contain rôles —star rôles. Composers pay scant attention to the fact that in opera it is the singers, or, in a word, in stage-plays it is the players, who are to be considered as the authors' chief aids to fame and fortune.

LOBE:—But, with all this working over, is not the loftier artistic spirit of dramatic works often lost? We have many plays with rôles such as you prefer, to which we can hardly ascribe a high artistic value.

LORTZING:—True enough! On the other hand, we also have plays whose high dramatic value we must recognize, and which nevertheless cannot maintain themselves on the stage just because they contain no rôles. When both requirements are combined—then, indeed, the poet has attained the loftiest goal, as the plays of our dramatists, Shakespeare, Goethe and Schiller, prove, both requirements being fulfilled in them. Such men, however, are of the rarest, and if the managements were permitted to give no plays but such as theirs—

LOBE (*interrupting him*):—So, in your opinion, anyone to whom the genius of a Shakespeare, Goethe, Schiller, Mozart, Beethoven, etc., is denied, should content himself with lesser undertakings? Might we not better say, in the interest of art, Rather let him who does not feel equal to the highest tasks, abstain altogether? What does a connoisseur care for mediocrity? (And as Lortzing greeted this question with a somewhat peculiar smile, Lobe suddenly realized what a snare he had set for himself, and hastily continued): It is hardly necessary to assure you that your own operas—

LORTZING (*interrupting him*):—Oh, old friend, no diplomatic finesse between you and me! The remark that my things are beneath mediocrity, cannot insult me, because it is true. But that such as I should refrain from production on that account, I cannot admit. Connoisseur? Oh yes, a fine title. How many of them do you think you could get together in Leipzig, or any other city? How many could you turn into regular theatregoers? And how many would agree in their opinions concerning the works of art? Is not Robert Schumann a musician of the highest capacity? Well, let him write an opera only for Mendelssohn and other similar connoisseurs. Would his music thoroughly satisfy these men? Would they agree in praise or blame for all the numbers? And besides—how long do you suppose a theatre would exist, in which only creations of the highest genius could be produced, and where the audiences should be composed of connoisseurs alone? You could not scrape together enough perfect works to fill a half-year's repertory, and the receipts from select audiences of connoisseurs would not pay the theatre manager for the oil in his lamps! It would be delightful if all art-works were perfect and all men were connoisseurs.

But the Lord has willed it otherwise. Human beings on this planet must have different capacities, different tastes, different education —but all should enjoy art so far as may be. Some of my operas give many honest souls pleasure for hours; with that I am satisfied.

Here, so far as Lobe gives it, the conversation between the two men breaks off. I have reproduced this portion of the important dialogue in extenso because the plain talk of the unassuming master seems, in my opinion, to outweigh a bulky compendium of theoretical reasoning. Only after one has carefully examined his texts and compared them with the originals, does one realize how much of his own personality Lortzing imparted to the revamped old comedies, and how he often so greatly varied their structure and casts that, in spite of a literal taking-over of some parts of the dialogue, the works in their present shape may be considered as his personal property. For nearly all the great dramatic poets—the Spaniards, Molière and Shakespeare beyond the rest—employed no other procedure in many of their pieces; as practical stage-folk they laid hold of good material left by their predecessors, retained the successful scenes, and completely rewrote the ineffective ones. Hence, numerous subjects, more especially those of a sprightly character, took on their definitive form only after the lapse of generations. That, of course, runs counter to the present craze for originality, when every individual would fain be an original genius of a wholly new type. One should consider, however, that it is not a wholly despicable feat when, without poetical pretensions, one can write an opera-book for oneself in good workmanlike style, as has been done in Germany, for example, by Kienzl ("Der Evangelimann"), in Italy by Leoncavallo ("Pagliacci"), and in France by Charpentier ("Louise").

4. Wagner's Procedure

This is most clearly explained in a letter written by the master to Carl Gaillard on Jan. 30th, 1844, in which he says: "I am really under no illusions concerning my avocation as a poet, and confess that it was only from necessity, because no good librettos were offered me, that I tried my hand at writing them. But now I should find it quite impossible to do so, for the following reason:— It is not my way of working to choose any subject, no matter what, turn it into verse, and then reflect how I shall write a suitable music for it. By adopting this method I should certainly be exposed to the disadvantage of having to warm over my first inspiration, something I could not do. But my mode of production is different. First of all, no subject has attraction for me except one that presents itself to me not only in its poetical, but also at the same time in its musical, significance. Before I begin to write a verse, or even to plan a scene, I am already intoxicated by the musical redolence of my creation; I have all the tones, all the characteristic motives, in my head, so that, when the verses are finished and the scenes arranged, for me the opera itself is completed, and the musical treatment in detail is more like a quiet, deliberate finishing job, the moment of creation proper having already preceded it. And for this purpose, besides, only such subjects can be selected as are suitable solely for musical treatment. I would never choose a subject that could be just as readily wrought into a spoken drama by some clever theatre poet. But I, as a musician, can select subjects and invent situations and contrasts which must ever remain foreign to the poet of the spoken drama. And just here, it would seem, is the parting of the ways between opera and drama, each thereafter tranquilly following its own path. If it is the task of the dramatic poet at the present time to cleanse and spiritualize the material interests of our epoch from a moral point of view, it is left to the opera-poet and composer to set free, as with a magic wand, that sacred soul of poetry that calls to us out of the sagas and stories of old, in all its rightful charm; for music offers us to this end a vehicle for combinations which are not at the command of the poet alone, particularly when our actors are taken into account."

In addition to the above he writes, in the "Mittheilung an meine Freunde": "In the case of 'Rienzi' it was still my idea only to write an 'opera'; to this end I sought after materials and, taking thought only for the opera, I borrowed them from finished poems which, as to form, were already constructed with artistic discrimination—a dramatic fairy tale by Gozzi, a drama by Shakespeare, and finally a novel by Bulwer-Lytton; these I adapted to the peculiar requirements of the opera. For 'Rienzi' . . . I elaborated . . . the material (as, considering the nature of an historical novel, was not practicable otherwise) with greater freedom, following the impressions it had made on me, and this in the guise in which I had seen it through the 'operaglass.' With 'The Flying Dutchman' I entered upon a new path, myself becoming the artistico-poetic upbuilder of this plot, given me only in a simple, rough sketch as a folk-legend. From that time, with regard to all my dramatic works, I was first of all a poet, and not until after the complete construction of the poem did I again become a musician. But I was a poet conscious, from the outset, of what music is capable of expressing. . . ."

So we see that Wagner, too, originally went to work like any good handicraftsman. It was only when he had acquired a sound theatrical technic and attained to the requisite mastery of both poetical and musical expression, that he could allow himself full liberty in the shaping of his poetico-musical conceptions. But there is one thing that we of to-day should clearly understand: Wagner's technic is purely individualistic—a technic that permits of renewed application only in case it again happens that dramatist and musician are united in one person of equally powerful endowment. Centuries of historical evolution were required before such a man could come forth, and it seems probable that an artist of like calibre will not again appear all too soon. This cannot prevent our learning from Wagner in the matter of technics whatever may be learned from him. But no one should attempt to imitate him. If all signs of the times are not deceptive, we are headed for an epoch in which, with strong emphasis on the element of melody, we shall draw nearer to the old opera-form, without renouncing the imperishable dramatic heritage won through Wagner. His attitude to the libretto-question with reference to young composers he once stated in conversation with Hans von Wolzogen: "When anyone lays before me the score of a newly composed opera, it means nothing at all to me; such progress has been made in the devices of harmonization, of the augmented triads, of instrumentation, and the general routine of modern composition, that one can feel sure beforehand not to find any special crudities or stupidities. But I ask to see the book of the opera; that shows me whether the man has a sense for dramatic poetry, and from it I can judge whether he has a gift for dramatic music, in case he succeeded in finding the right musical expression for his text—which, indeed, very rarely happens."

THE LITERARY OPERA

The Strauss-Debussy Procedure

Concerning the disadvantageousness of this procedure, discarded in the end by its two chief representatives, no doubt prevails among competent judges, despite the sensational success of "Pelléas" and "Salome." It is certain that no literary drama, however abridged in form, can provide a suitable foundation for an opera; in every situation where the music, in its essential nature, demands wider expansion, the poem is found wanting, and the musician is forced to set a quantity of unmusical detail to music simply because the literary plan of the action renders it imperative. Nowadays, as we all know, one can compose (as some term it) anything whatever, even playbills, as the jovial Udel Quartet once proved by their delicious setting of a "Freischütz" playbill to themes from Weber. Unhappily, the spiritual bond is usually missing in a poem so harmonized (as it were) with hide and hair. Such a poem is available, in a higher sense, only when written (or at least adapted) with a special view to composition. The Strauss-Debussy procedure is, to be sure, comprehensible in view of the dearth of really good librettists, and for the reason that hardly a noteworthy poet of our day would be willing to undertake the thankless task of constructing an opera-book. The good old times when a Beaumarchais could sneer: "Aujourd'hui ce qui ne vaut pas la peine d'être dit, on le chante," are gone forever, and therefore it is high time that composers should acquire that minimum of dramatic insight without which they court dire disaster on the stage.

Now arises the important question:

Must the opera-composer be his own librettist?

To this we may reply, even to Wagnerians of the strictest school, with the tranquillizing assurance that, in the opinion of Wagner himself, he does *not* need to be. Wagner did, indeed, constantly extol the union of poet and musician in one person as the ideal case; yet the history of opera shows, more especially with Mozart and Verdi, that ideally perfect artworks may also issue from the union of two persons. Ask yourself candidly: Do you find any point of perfection wanting in "The Marriage of Figaro," taken as a whole, such as signalizes (say) "Die Meistersinger von Nürnberg"? To my mind, you will not, provided that "Figaro" be performed according to the original Italian version, not contenting oneself with some translation which, at best, must subvert the marvelous unity between language and music. Wagner himself, in his discussion with Rossini, plainly stated what course composers ought to pursue. Rossini held the requirement, that the composer should be his own librettist, for "well-nigh unrealizable," whereupon Wagner replied that composers could just as well take up the study of legend and history as that of counterpoint, and in so doing would surely find a subject suited to their individuality. "And if they lack skill or experience for planning the dramatic action, would it not be possible for them to call upon some competent dramaturgist, together with whom they could work? Besides, there have been but few dramatic composers who have not instinctively shown remarkable literary and poetical talent on occasion, by altering the position of the text or the planning of a scene at their pleasure, grasping its feeling and significance better than the librettist."

Thus Wagner recommends to all those who cannot be their own librettists that they should work together with a playwright—*nota bene*, not with any given so-called "poet." While recommending the method adopted by Gluck and Mozart, he lays chief emphasis on the stage-craft of the coadjutor, who must be thoroughly familiar with dramatic construction. Accordingly, there remain for the present-day dramatic composer only three possible procedures, namely:

1. If you are a universal genius like Wagner, you will know of your own accord precisely what to do.

2. If you possess a stage-routine like Lortzing's, you too will need no dramaturgic instruction, but you must have a certain command of language. And, having this, which enables you to write an opera-book for yourself, you still may find the following suggestions quite useful.

3. If you are a musician pure and simple, and still feel an unconquerable urge toward dramatic activity (*nota bene*, a hankering after fat royalties will not, in itself, suffice), it is necessary for you to gain familiarity with the elements of dramaturgy, so that you may find the right man for the elaboration of your books and, when you have found him, that you may put your finger on the weak spots in the construction. It is—I am going to betray this secret of the handicraft—much wiser to have your whole book in correct shape before you begin setting it to music, than to be forced later by stage-managers and conductors to make dozens of cuts and to waste time in rewriting. For purely musical imperfections are more easily corrected than dramatic faults which vitiate the entire structure of the score.

CHAPTER II

The Subject of an Opera

The lore of the divining-rod, which discovers to the initiated, by its magnetic pull, here the living waters and there the hidden gold, is no mere illusion of sense. There are persons so sensitively endowed that they can find hidden treasure. In view of recent investigations science itself has had to renounce its prejudice against the water-finding rod, and that there are men who can trace the buried gold of times long past, and remould it into new forms, is something that we see repeated again and again in the poetry of all times and peoples. The last great example in the realm of the musical drama was Richard Wagner, who exhumed the wondrous legends of prehistoric times from their epic dust, and gave them back to the world in the purely human guise of a refined dramatic form.

But (I hear someone object) we are no geniuses in the class of a Wagner. He has preëmpted the finest of the ancient legends, and anyhow, the interest in legends is exhausted.

Therefore, how am I to find a good theme for an opera?

Answer:—Just as one finds the right kind of wife!

Yes, but one must know how to do that, too!

Verily, one must indeed know how to do that; it is even more difficult than finding a theme for an opera. For either, one must possess some *amor fati.* The true dramatist finds his best subjects without premeditation, and he will never suffer for want of them—rather from an overabundance. Any old or new book that happens to fall into our hands, makes our heart beat higher; some unostentatious incident of the daily news, unnoticed by millions of readers, is the cosmic cell of a wondrous creation; or some personal experience strikes a creative root into our being.

Once your theme is chosen, O young musician! rest assured that it will inspire you to the best that your Muse has to give you. But, ere you give bonds to eternity, take heedful counsel with yourself whether in your theme you find not only your own inspiration but a means for enravishing others, as well. Consider, that a drama, unlike a lyric or an epic, may not slumber long in script until at last, glorious as on the first day, it shall slowly and gradually come into its own. Consider, that it is your task to affect at one moment many dissimilar souls.

The foremost condition is an action full of variety and suspense. Failing of success on the stage, without leaving a vivid impression on any auditors of high or low degree, a drama has missed its aim, even though it contain in detail the loftiest dramatic and musical beauties. The greatest dramatist of all ages and nations did not think it beneath his dignity to write such pieces as "As You Like It" and "Twelfth Night." And Wagner's worldly-wise Hans Sachs likewise opines:

> You strive to please the people:
> Well then, if I were you,
> I think I'd let them tell me
> How *they* like what you do!

This is loftier wisdom than ponderous tomes can supply, and an appeal to the plain commonsense of the public has never, in the long run, yet failed of effect. Therefore, O young musician, my advice is this: When your first poetical transports have run their course, and you are quite clear as to the choice of your subject and the practicability of its dramatic exploitation, write out a short sketch of the action, a concise relation of the several acts, and lay it before some theatrical expert— either a competent dramatic poet on whose discretion you can rely, or rather some director or stage-manager (*nota bene*, a theatre conductor is seldom a dependable judge). This

theatrical expert will then either cool off your
enthusiasm for your theme considerably, and
possibly convince you of its unsuitableness by
practical objections, or he will—and then you
may think yourself very fortunate—declare the
plot effective as a whole, but advise you to
alter certain details of the plan (most likely
the act-closes). Do not be obstinate when
confronted by a trusted and friendly adviser;
give his suggestions earnest consideration even
in case, at first blush, they seem to stand
your well-devised plot on its head. Afterwards you will generally discover that the
man was not so entirely wrong, even where
you do not follow his suggestions literally and
feel moved to make certain changes only.
You need not regard an expert as infallible.
Even directors and stage-managers can make
mistakes, and many an old hand has dreaded
failure in the case of pieces that won success,
and *vice versa*. So listen to several men;
should they, independently of one another,
tell you the same thing, be convinced that
you are in the wrong. Should they disagree,
ponder which opinion you prefer to follow.
But lay aside all conceit and self-complacency
until your dramatic qualifications have been
approved by the public. Reflect, that the
public is the sole court of last resort which is
to decide the fate of your work; no directorial

favor, no brilliant reviews, can avert your dismissal from the stage after a few performances, if the piece does not "draw," that is, does not attract paying audiences. True enough, eminent masterworks have before this fallen flat because at first they were not understood by the public, or—as really happens quite often—because of imperfect presentation; but, in the end, every truly genuine dramatic talent has won public favor. Nothing is truer than the old stage-saying: "The individual is an ass, the crowd is the voice of God." And as someone rightly complimented Voltaire on being the wittiest man of his time, he observed: "There is somebody who is wittier than Voltaire—everybody." My word for it—every piece that is a real success on the stage possesses some peculiar theatrical quality by reason of which it gained success. Do not be arrogant and say: "I can't see why this hotchpotch succeeded and my masterwork failed." Rather, examine studiously the good points of this "hotchpotch," and ask yourself whether your work, after all, may possibly not possess these qualities. Musicians and conductors are apt to judge one-sidedly from the orchestra score (many critics do the same, sad to say!); the audience and stagefolk, however, care only for the stage-effect; no matter how superficial it is, the success of the piece is assured. The fine distinction between *theatrical* (i.e., sensational) and *dramatic* (i.e., effective on the stage in the higher sense) is recognized by none among the stagefolk. As the architecture of a building is based on established constructive considerations, in disregard whereof the structure would crash in upon itself, the drama, too, has its established technic, which is not a demonstration of any abstract theory, but a living branch of artistry continually enriched by new inventions.

An opera-book rests, for the most part, upon the same constructive foundations as the spoken drama, and still there may be found many a deviation necessitated by the alliance with music, so that it is not altogether easy and simple to apply the general rules of dramaturgy unconditionally in this peculiar sphere.

CHAPTER III

LAWS OF CONSTRUCTION

Between the joyful discovery of an operatic subject and its definitive adaptation for composition there is a long road to travel, and this road leads, first of all, through the territory of substantial, workmanlike technic, such as all great dramatists from Shakespeare to Richard Wagner have possessed. What we call technic is, in the last analysis, merely the systematic application of those rules which guarantee a certain stage-effect on the audience. Technic therefore can never be gray theory; it is ever the golden fruit of the tree of life. Although it is thus, as to its better part, mostly gained by experience, it must be systematically practised in the outset in certain elementary concepts; otherwise the beginner would employ too much valuable time in learning experimentally from individual cases over which, viewed as members of a system, he would gain the mastery in brief space. Buffon remarked: "Art is mathematics; great effects are produced by simple means well combined." And Maupassant wrote to Vauclaire: "Genius is nothing but enduring patience." Certainly, one cannot get along with technic alone, but without it one will never be anything but a bungler, even when one has a superfluity of "splendid ideas." "Craftsmanship acquired within limitations must always precede all life, all action, all art. To know and practise one thing well is a higher education than half-knowledge of many things," declares Goethe. Great art-works can be created only by the reciprocal action of knowledge and imagination, never by imagination or knowledge alone. And hardly any other branch of art is so dependent on this reciprocal action, as the musical drama. This is the ultimate source of Wagner's tremendous effectiveness.

The dilettante throws off his thoughts on paper—they might have been otherwise. The imaginative artist has positive ideas that hold their own, yet do not carry conviction. Only the finished master conquers his audience; he leaves is no way of escape—the art-work casts its spell over even recalcitrant spirits. But victory can be won only by a work whose raw material has been shaped by the hand of a master who has all technical devices at command.

Suppose your subject luckily found; now arises the question, What shall be the form?—for a subject is never available in the same form that it bore when discovered. So it makes an essential difference, whether you found your subject already dramatized, or in an amplified epic form, or merely in the shape of an anecdote to be elaborated. Three examples follow:

1. For "The Marriage of Figaro" Da Ponte utilized the finished comedy by Beaumarchais in such a way that his libretto follows the drama almost scene by scene, so that considerable changes, cuts, and additions to the structure, were made only in certain passages whose recasting was imperatively demanded.

2. For "Carmen" the librettists, Meilhac and Halévy, utilized the full-fledged novel by Mérimée, which furnished them with a wealth of detail; although drama and story, each after its own kind, occasionally show wide divergences.

3. The book of "Aida" was derived from a short anecdote communicated by the famous Egyptologist Mariette-Bey. Camille du Locle wrote a dramatic sketch based on this incident, and Ghislanzoni versified this sketch for Verdi.[1]

[1] Compare "A Genetic Study of the Aida Libretto" by Edgar Istel (*Musical Quarterly*, Jan., 1917—III, 1), and "The Othello of Verdi and Shakespeare" (*ibid.*, July, 1916—II, 3). The same author will publish later an essay on "Carmen" (novel and opera) in the same periodical.

It is clear that, from a purely dramatico-technical standpoint, the framing of the "Aida" libretto was decidedly more difficult than that of the "Carmen" book, and that the latter, in turn, necessarily gave more trouble than the "Figaro" text. But even the difficulties that Da Ponte met with should by no means be underrated. The "Figaro" book operates nowadays like the egg of Columbus—every wretched scribbler thinks he can create its like out of some one among the many French comedies, which assuredly offer an excellent working basis.

There is no *master*piece of world-literature that has not already been "worked over" into an opera-book. The really good operatic themes (Shakespeare's, in particular) have long since found their definitive musical setting, and it is time now that *master*works should cease to be made the happy hunting ground of the librettists' art. Lortzing recommended "unremembered middle-class" plays for adaptation. It is true that really well-constructed stage-pieces—unless they are mere fads of a period—do not generally disappear so tracelessly from the scene, excepting when some ill fortune attended their first performance. The opera-composer who has been so fortunate as to unearth such a drama, must fix his attention on certain points to be noted directly. In any event, he has before him a real stage-play, wrought out and subdivided, and in this respect has the advantage over any rivals who are obliged to work up into dramatic form some narrative or mere anecdote. An advantage, to be sure, of somewhat superficial sort, with less of difficulty and brainwork. Intrinsically, the finding of a finished drama may work to his disadvantage, when his imagination is too strongly attracted by the ready-made scenario and may refuse here and there to act independently. To me, at least, it has often seemed as if the eggshells (if I may so express it) of the original form had a tendency to bob up fragmentarily even in the well-prepared dish. However, such fragments of a former dramatic dishing-up are as nothing in comparison with those remnants of an epic style that so often cling to dramas whose authors were not skillful enough to transform the borrowed narrative into a genuine drama. The "Carmen" book is noteworthy as a felicitous example of cleverest adaptation more especially because it is not only finely calculated for stage-effect, but also offers the composer inexhaustible opportunities for musical development. For practical use by the majority of our composers we can assume, in a general way, that they will base the construction of their books either on stage-plays or on well-rounded narratives; the third method, namely, free invention based on meagre material (to which, to a certain extent, all of Wagner's works from "The Flying Dutchman" onward belong), is practicable only for genius, and therefore may as well be left out of consideration. That shall not prevent us, however, from examining his operas analytically, "Tannhäuser," "Lohengrin" and "Die Meistersinger" being, in particular, *chefs-d'œuvre* of dramaturgic art. In "The Flying Dutchman" various details of construction are not wholly successful; the "Ring," as a work of gigantic proportions and often not impeccable dramaturgically, occupies an exceptional position; in "Tristan," excepting the wonderfully constructed first act, the epic ingredients of the source are so strongly in evidence that the dramatic structure cannot be held up as a model. In "Parsifal" also, taken as a whole, that mighty dramatic energy is lacking which the master possessed at the zenith of his creative powers.

Now, on approaching the actual technical problem of construction, the artist must, to begin with, keep one fundamental requirement well in view. Let him *visualize* his work, that is, let him continually bear in mind that whatever he creates has not only to be *heard*, but, above all, to be *seen*. In effect, the *action* of a good opera must be thoroughly intelligible, even when the greater part of the *text* is not understood by the hearers. This dictum sounds self-evident, but is by no means so in fact, as hundreds of unsuccessful dramas and operas have demonstrated. The dramatic poet himself is constantly tempted to narrate, to describe, to revel in high-sounding words, to indulge in clever discussion and soul-analysis. All this is not merely useless, but hurtful, and, when music is superadded, positively disastrous. Do not forget, first of all, that any prolixity, however slight, in the book will be prolonged, musically considered, to at least thrice its length, and that any musical over-extension sensibly impedes the flow of the dramatic development. The audience is bored —the worst that can happen in the theatre. The onlooker should follow the happenings on the stage with eager interest, and such interest can be sustained only by extreme conciseness, by avoidance of all superfluous verbiage. Withal, a libretto cannot be short enough; only where some essential breathing-space occurs in the action, offering a possibility for musical expansion, may it say to the moment: "Ah, stay a while, thou art so fair." If it does so elsewhere, straightway the demon of tedium has it by the neck. And, of course, what is required of the poet is equally required of the composer:—no superfluous interludes, which only clog the action and embarrass the actors; no showing-off with orchestral coloration and thematic combination when the action is inexorably hastening forward. Compose, not with your ears alone, but with your eyes, too! Don't let the music run ahead of the stageplay, as even very celebrated composers have done, on occasion. One horrible example —a composer whose stage-successes, thanks to highly sensational propaganda, have been very clamorous in recent years, but who is more of a musician than dramatist, wrote long orchestral interludes for his most famous work. When the stage-manager, at the first stage-rehearsal before the première, asked him what he had had in mind while composing them, he answered "Oh, you may do whatever you please." It was naturally out of the question to infuse any dramatic life into these interludes, so they had to be "padded" with improvised stageplay. From which it may be seen, that the composer in question has not yet out-Wagnered Wagner. With Wagner and with all genuine dramatic composers, Gluck in particular, not one superfluous episodic measure can be found. In fact, as an experienced stage-manager assured me, one may look upon a composer's interludes as a touchstone of his dramatic ability. No expert is in doubt as to whether a given interlude is seen, or simply heard.

Hence, the first and most vital requirement for the musical drama is, that it bear the test of sight. Almost all the other laws of dramatic representation are to be derived from this one. Imagine yourself seated among the audience; bethink you, that the finest discourses and instrumental combinations excogitated at your writing-table are, when viewed from the auditorium, as nothing in comparison with the living drama on the· stage. Never fancy yourself the conductor, but always the stage-manager, of your opera, while writing the poem or the music. Or, still better, imagine yourself on the stage, and ask how you yourself would play or sing this scene or that; then, and only then, will your piece take on life. Reflect, that on the lifeless paper you can give only in outline that which others have to transmute into warm life—that which, in turn, is to delight, elevate, transport, or possibly only "amuse," still others who have no conception of "the score." Do not turn up your nose at the art of the dramatist who merely "amuses." It is harder to amuse the public uninterruptedly for an hour, than to bore them for three hours with "lofty" art. "Tous les genres sont bons, hors le genre ennuyeux," observed Voltaire in his preamble to a comedy. Anyone becomes tiresome who ceases to be perspicuous. In his "Über das Operndichten und -Komponieren im besonderen" Wagner, in the closing years of his life, let fall golden words concerning perspicuity which, unhappily, have too seldom been taken to heart: "I would advise any dramatic composer of a tendency like mine never, above all things, to adopt a text before he has made sure that the action, and the characters carrying on the action, for some reason excite in him, as a musician, a lively interest. Then let him take a good look at some particular character which, for the moment, he finds most attractive; if she wears a mask—off with it! if she is clad in the garb of a costumer's figurine—down with it! Now let him take his stand in a twilight nook whence he can see only the glance of her eye; if this speaks to him, her form itself may now take on a movement which possibly affrights him—but which he has to view unresisting; at last her lips quiver, she opens her mouth, and a spirit-voice tells him something genuinely true, wholly intelligible, and yet so unheard-of (as, mayhap, the Stone-Guest and the Page Cherubin told Mozart) that—in the hearing he awakes from his dream. All is lost to sight; but in his mental ear the tones linger—a new idea is born."

From the requirement of perspicuity is necessarily derived that of limitation to the absolutely essential. "To present essentials, but in the guise of accidentals, that is the whole secret of the dramatic style," observes Hebel. And Lessing ("Hamburgische Dramaturgie," 82. Stück) writes: "The simpler a machine is, the fewer springs, wheels and weights it has, the more perfect it is." The plot must be reduced to the simplest possible form. All epic redundances must be unsparingly lopped off; every single incident of the action must be definitely connected with the main plot or, if it cannot be organically combined, set aside. The very first sketch must show clearly the course of the play in its fundamental lines. This limitation applies in like manner to the number of characters and also to the number of acts and changes of scene. **Chief rule**: As few characters as any way possible, and limitation of the persons taking no active part to the lowest figure. With regard to the framing of the libretto of "The Merry Wives of Windsor" Nicolai wrote in his diary: "After going over it once more, I altered and simplified the design, eliminating the character of *Mrs. Quickly* (who plays such an important part in Shakespeare's comedy), and doing away with several other characters which would greatly overburden the cast of an opera or render it quite unmanageable, for each additional rôle in the opera usually means one more difficulty in performances." Let each subordinate character represent a clean-cut type. Model examples are *Kurwenal* and *Brangäne* in "Tristan und Isolde." A lesser dramatist, or a poet of epic propensities, would have invented a whole retinue of serving-folk for "Tristan"; Wagner contented himself with two types.—**Further,** if you can, get along without episodical figures who vanish without a trace after brief coöperation. Give each of your characters a "grateful" part which is organically intertwined with the main lines of the action.

Moreover, compress your action into the smallest number of acts. After "The Flying Dutchman" (which, in reality, is only a one-act opera) Wagner contented himself with three acts, though he made it possible in the first act of "Götterdämmerung" and the third act of "Die Meistersinger" only by the application of force. In general, however, it may be said that good opera-subjects can always be brought within the compass of three or, at the outside, four acts ("Carmen," and most of Verdi's operas, have four). It depends, of course, entirely upon the length of the acts. If you would keep your audience "fresh" (in this point Wagner sinned greatly) an act should not last longer than from one hour to an hour and a half. Three acts of one hour each, or four acts of from a half-hour to three-quarters of an hour, with fifteen-minute intervals, may be considered as the maximum for an opera-evening, excepting possibly during some festival season. In no case ought one forcibly to expand a one-act subject so as to fill an entire evening. Nowadays the mass of operagoers do not enjoy sitting through more than four acts, and after all one goes to the theatre for the enjoyment, not as the slave, of art. The form of the five-act Grand Opera, as affected by Meyerbeer, is now probably given up for good because of its length. Restrict changes of scene within the acts as far as possible. Only the modern sectional or revolving stages, which are not at the command of all theatres, permit of frequent and rapid scenic changes. Scene-shifting in the course of an act is at best disturbing to the mood, however cleverly it may be bridged over by musical interludes. With every scenic shift or change a piece begins anew for the audience. On no account should more than one change of scene occur in an act, and then only when there is a peremptory reason for it. Only unskillful dramatists declare that they cannot get along without frequent changes of scene. On reflection one usually finds a surprisingly easy way out of the difficulty. Do not cite Shakespeare's example to the contrary, for his stage was innocent of the modern impedimenta of scenic decoration, and his dramatic technic (often related to that of our moving pictures) could therefore be different from that obtaining at present. The far too frequent scene-changes in Mozart's operas require a revolving or sliding stage, otherwise the numerous pauses destroy the illusion. And when some new construction is insisted on, consider how long its setting-up will require. You will do best to consult a stage-manager, who can tell you precisely how many minutes will be needed (more especially by the ladies, if with change of costume), for a change of scene. Adapt your musical interlude accordingly; but don't compose after the recipe "Now I have only 3 minutes' worth of music— where can I get another 7 minutes' worth?" Start your interlude as nearly *fortissimo* as possible (for at the beginning the noises of scene-shifting are at their height), and conceive it at the outset in so broad a form that it will need no expansion later, otherwise the "patching" will be painfully evident. The matter is simplest when a scene occupying only the front of the stage is changed to one occupying its entire depth, or the reverse. In the former case a great part of the scenery can be placed before the change; in the latter, the rear decorations can be easily and swiftly masked behind a new drop scene. When both scenes require the full depth of the stage, the change naturally demands a much longer time. The above practical suggestions are often left out of the calculation, but their timely application will save much work and worry. Even Schiller once remarked: "I should be so unphilosophical as to exchange everything I know about elementary æsthetics for one empirical advantage, one trick of the trade."

How the first draught ought to be framed can be most clearly and profitably learned from Wagner's sketches for "Die Meistersinger," "Tristan," and "Parsifal." It is in the three sketches to "Die Meistersinger" that one can most readily follow the progress of the work; and still, although in these we already find the externals of the action established in their entirety with hardly a break, how weak and colorless it all appears contrasted with the lifelike organization of the essential plot, which became manifest only in the complete working-out of the sketches. Just this point characterizes the real master; he is not satisfied with his work until he has exploited the ultimate possibilities of the subject.

The choice of a title is very important; above all, it should be short, and designed to fit into a playbill—for poster-effect; not over three or four words. Keep the fact in view that the title should whet the public appetite, but without revealing anything essential. Make up all the titles you can think of, and then, with your friends' help, choose the most effective one. "The title must not be a bill of fare," says Lessing. "The less it reminds of the plot, the better."

It is advisable not to undertake to write out the sketch before you are quite clear in your own mind as to the course of the action. One should sit in the centre of the dramatic web like a spider; then the figures of the drama will grow more and more lifelike, and must move the author's soul by day and by night as if they were living beings. They must continually inspire new ideas and combinations in their creator's brain, till all at once, sooner or later, all the personages and situations stand out so distinctly and tangibly that he can rid his teeming fancy of the superfluity of images only by imprisoning them in writing. It is particularly helpful to explain the course of the action orally to some friendly expert in stage-matters; then the most difficult problem may find ready solution in conversation, and unimagined possibilities present themselves. Now—take pen in hand, but not before. This advice is based on a good reason—speech is more true to life than writing. Whoever trusts his pen rather than his conceptive faculty, will never produce a genuine drama.

Now, from the very start, keep steadily in view the three chief points in the drama:

1. The Exposition.
2. The Development.
3. The Dénouement.

Experience shows the central portion, the development, to be the least difficult. The exposition is extremely difficult, and can be carried out to perfection only by a master of the art. Most difficult of all, and decisive for the fate of the piece, is the dénouement. Most dramas "fall off" after the climax. The hearer's interest relaxes, and the effect of the piece is destroyed. Therefore, first of all, fix your attention upon the framing of a good close. This close, however, must not be pieced on as a mere afterthought, but must appear as a necessary consequence of all that has gone before. Of similar, and not much less importance, is the close of the first act; if by that time the spectator has not been "warmed up," if his interest is not sufficiently aroused, it will be no easy matter to overcome his indifference later; besides, boredom in the theatre, like interest, has an uncanny way of infecting others. Nietzsche once remarked, "One feels his neighborhood"—that is, the mood of the majority in the audience imposes itself on the rest, even on recalcitrant spirits.

If his subject is good for anything, even an author of comparatively slight ability will succeed in shaping his climax effectively. On the other hand, supposing we have three acts, if the middle act-close fails of effect the whole piece may be given up for lost. Hardly one work can be named that improves toward the end after beginning and middle have failed. Moral:—Be extremely careful with your very first lay-out of the piece.

Strange as it may sound to the beginner, comic subjects are decidedly more difficult to work up than tragic ones. And why? Because the tragic action, after adequate exposition, carries on of itself, so to speak, for in this case, once the fundamental mood is established, the approaching catastrophe overspreads even the weaker passages of the drama with the gloomy shadow of death; because the tragic hero's career must end with his destruction, and nothing else can be expected. *Per contra,* the comic subject demands new humoristic imaginings at every turn; a single dull scene may have such a tiresome effect that the audience does not get over it. The difference between tragedy and comedy might be defined as that between "fearful suspense" and "hopeful suspense." But the basic laws of suspense are the same in both, as, in the musical cadence, the Dominant is the same in major as in minor. Moreover, there are many possible forms of dénouement, and of these the one most provocative of suspense should be chosen; the author should not show his hand too early, but astonish his audience at the last moment by a solution that the cleverest among the spectators would scarcely have hit upon. Sardou, assuredly one of the most artful exponents of dramatic technique, witnessed the failure of his ill-planned dramatic firstling. What did he do? He went to the country, taking along a number of Scribe's masterworks with which he was still unfamiliar; read of each only the first act, then sketched a continuation of the action, and finally compared his as yet bungling attempts with the skillful dénouements of the original. Thus he at last acquired his own never-failing technical mastery. Scribe himself, it is said, forgot in later years the action of his earlier works—no matter for surprise, considering his wholesale productivity —but liked to attend performances of such old pieces. When affairs grew highly complicated, he would laughingly exclaim: "Now I'm really curious to see how I disentangled myself!"

While elaborating your plot you must, above all, see to it that the form of the action is truly dramatic.

What is "dramatic"? It is almost impossible to answer that question concisely. The late Freiherr Alfred von Berger, director of the Vienna Hofburg Theatre, wittily observed in his spirited "Dramaturgische Vorträge" (Dramaturgic Discourses) that the attempts to state the mysterious essence of dramatic art in a formula not infrequently reminded him of the attempts of the Wise Men of Gotham to dip up the sunlight in pitchers and to catch it in artfully contrived mousetraps, so as to transport it into their dark townhall.

But even Berger's own definition advances us not a step in practice, for it turns about in a circle. One might just as well say, "What has dramatic effect, is dramatic." With no pretension of doing better than others have done, I venture, from a purely practical standpoint, to define the nature of dramatic art thus briefly:

An unbroken chain of growingly intensified situations, resulting in actions which consistently follow one after the other, and leading up to a striking dénouement, is dramatic.

It seems to me that in this definition the principal difficulties in the technics of the drama are likewise suggested:

1. The situations of which the drama is constructed must form an unbroken chain with correspondingly growing intensification. Such continuous intensification is the essence of the drama, failing which it never interests. But only such an intensification is effective which is part and parcel of the general plot. The situations must follow each other in unbroken succession, i.e., the auditor must be informed betimes concerning all essential points of the drama, more especially antecedent events, otherwise there will be an annoying break in his apprehension of the plot. For the same reason, nothing essential should occur between acts that is not immediately explained. The imagination of the auditors themselves will correctly interpret subordinate episodes. Situations that do not lead up to actions, fall quite as flat as mere talk and analyses of feeling.

2. One chief rule for the drama is, not to present a desultory succession of scenes like those of the "movies," but rather an organic, logical development of the entire action out of the germ-cells of the drama as they are set forth by the characters and in the situations of the principals at the beginning of the play. A question of the highest importance is, at what point of time the drama shall commence. If it begins too early, time is wasted in ex-

plaining petty details; if too läte, the exposition is overweighted.

3. Climax and dénouement are the goals toward which the action must unswervingly pursue its course. These two points may either (as in the newest dramatic technic) coincide at the close, or the climax may occur in the midst of the play, the action then following a downward curve until the dénouement, which must necessarily be striking. Which course to take, in any given case, depends on the subject. Formulas fitting each individual case are non-existent. It is, naturally, most effective when the action "intensifies" up to the close.

These important bases being established, let us take up the difficult art of the "opening" and preparation—the Exposition.

"Tell me how you 'open' your play, and I will tell you what kind of dramatist you are," one might say to any author before the rise of the curtain or before reading his opening scenes. In fact, there is nothing in which the beginner so instantly differentiates himself from the "old hand," as in the difficult art of beginning. For, as to its words, the beginning is seldom quite clearly understood by the hearer, and must also give the musician an opportunity for deploying his motives, whereby not only the so-called leading-motives

are meant (one can make shift without them!),
but those hidden motives of action that the
musician alone can typify. (Consider, for
example, in Act I of "Die Walküre," whose
opening is masterly, how much is told by
means of music alone, what significant intimate relations, nowhere disclosed in the
words of the drama, are here revealed through
music and dumb-show.) In his "Oper und
Drama" Wagner says: "The characteristic
difference between word-poet and tone-poet
consists in this:—That the word-poet con-
centrates infinitely dispersed elements of
action, emotion, and expression, perceptible
only by the intellect, on a single point that
brings them as closely as possible into touch
with our feelings; whereas the tone-poet has
to expand this elemental concentration to
the fullest expression of its emotional content."
This concentration which Wagner demands
of the poet is, however, nowhere more difficult of achievement than at the opening of
the drama.

At the beginning one should ask, first of
all, What is it absolutely essential for the
spectator to know? Clearly, the answer to
this question depends upon what precedes
the rise of the curtain. The less that has to
be told about antecedent events, the better
is the subject (e.g., "Carmen"). For every

important incident occurring before the rise
of the curtain must be somehow interwoven
with the action—must be set before the
audience. The more these epic elements are
translated into actions, the more animated
the play becomes. Heinrich Laube, one of
the greatest theatrical experts of all times,
always paid most scrupulous attention to the
staging of the opening scenes: "And nobody
ever made the exposition so telling, as Laube."
Take, for instance, the complicated ante-
cendent history of "Tristan und Isolde,"
which in part is not cleared up until the
second and third acts (to explain it fully in
the first act would have overburdened the
action). But in how masterly fashion is the
story of Isolde's past here detailed, as it were,
bit by bit. An unskilled dramatist would
have let Brangäne ask, at the outset, "How
was it then, in truth, 'twixt thee and Tristan"?
—whereupon Isolde, as in duty bound, would
have told an endlessly tedious tale. Wagner
transports us at once *in medias res.* Already,
in the seemingly artless ditty of the Young
Sailor, which at first blush merely impresses a
mood, there is hidden a good bit of "exposition"—voyage eastward from Ireland to the
homeland of the crew; longing of a forsaken
Irish maiden, characterized as a "wilde minnige
Maid." This song of the Young Sailor,

sung wholly without allusive intent, but felt as a mock by Isolde, the "wildly lovelorn" Irish maiden, unconstrainedly gives the initial impulse to the dialogue between Isolde and Brangäne, so essential for explaining what had gone before. Here I cannot undertake the task of analyzing the opening of "Tristan" in detail; I would only point out how the very first and apparently casual words of the drama may—and must—convey important facts. The most important matters of all ought not to be set at the beginning, for special reasons; the onlooker must be given a certain length of time to "make himself at home" in the play. The "first aid" to this end is the overture, which should. not be devised merely for the introduction of the principal thematic material of the music (since any given potpourri of any desired melodies would answer that purpose), but must attune the hearer to the mood, the spirit, of the work; of this sort the preludes to "Lohengrin," "Tristan," "Die Meistersinger" and "Parsifal" are wonderful examples, and also Mozart's overtures, among which the one to "Figaro" is a familiar example of an overture without a single theme in common with its opera, but none the less induces that mood of genial gayety which is proper to a good interpretation of the masterwork. The recent fashion of raising the curtain after a brief pre-

lude of a few measures, is not always to be
approved; the hearer is often not sufficiently
"warmed up" to enter instantly into the spirit
of the opening scene, and in theatres where
late-comers are not excluded, disturbances are
likely to arise which spoil the enjoyment of
the beginning opera for more punctual auditors.
Preferable to the very few introductory measures now in vogue is a real overture which,
though short, creates the atmosphere of the
coming drama, as in the case of "Carmen"
and "Aida." We have dwelt upon this point
because the overture or prelude forms, as it
were, the very first exposition of the musical
drama; besides, the manner in which the
musician begins has an important bearing
on the construction of the book. The overture
may be said to take the place of the Prologue
in the antique drama, just as the orchestra, to
a degree, replaces the antique Chorus. The
modern prologue usual since Shakespeare, and
without connection with the action, is merely
an address by the poet; in opera it has been
successfully employed but once (by Leoncavallo in "Pagliacci"), and can be used in
the rarest instances, when the subject is
peculiarly favorable. The rule is, therefore,
that immediately following overture or prelude
the rising curtain discloses the scene. Now
we must not forget that at this moment the

attention of a large majority of the spectators—
especially of those unacquainted with the
piece—is fastened on the stage-picture, so
that what is said or sung is just now not of the
first importance; rather should the spectator
have time to scrutinize the scene of action and
the participating personages at his leisure.
An author who loses sight of this fact, and
starts in with some material bit of dialogue,
will discover to his sorrow that all his trouble
was wasted—that no one understood the
beginning. In the spoken drama, which, besides, usually suffers even more than the opera
from disquieting restlessness among the audience, one commonly has recourse to "padding"
with unimportant talk of general application,
leading into the more significant dialogue only
after some minutes. In opera the somewhat
conventional, but not wholly unpractical,
method is to start with a chorus whose sole
business it is to illustrate musically the time,
the place, and the mood, thereafter vanishing
from the scene. Nowadays, of course, this
procedure can be adopted only when such a
chorus can be introduced quite naturally and
unconstrainedly, and in that case it helps us
out of a certain embarrassment; consider how
admirably the chorus of the idly seated soldiers
of the watch characterizes the general situation at the beginning of "Carmen," or how

significantly the chorus at the opening of "Der Freischütz" intervenes in the action after the close of their number. In case the chorus takes no important part in the action during the course of the play, it is better to forgo its coöperation entirely, especially as chorus-operas, on account of the numerous rehearsals, are in disfavor with our stage-managements. Another way out of the difficulty, exquisitely employed by Wagner at the opening of "Tann-häuser," is the dance. Its placing in the opera at the beginning of an act is doubtless better justified, dramatically, than the formerly favored injection into a dramatic scene which is thereby brought to a standstill. And still other possibilities present themselves, among which the above-noted song of the Young Sailor at the opening of "Tristan," and the trio of the Rhine-daughters at the beginning of "Rheingold," may be cited as ingenious variations of the old opera-plan. The chorale with which "Die Meistersinger" opens shows us how that plan may be fruitfully modified; and the opening scene portraying Walter's love for Evchen and her reciprocation thereof shows how, without a single word, only by gesture and orchestral interludes, so important a fact can be most admirably revealed. So mark this point: At the beginning of the first act (and preferably at the beginning of each succeeding act) something ought to stand which, while organically connected with the main plot, must not be of such fundamental importance that the hearer has to take heed of every word. If you dislike the stereotyped chorus, you will probably do better with a pantomimic scene after Wagner's pattern, or at least with a scene where there is more action than dialogue (e.g., beginning of "Figaro"). Not until the spectator's curiosity regarding the characters, decorations and costumes has been satisfied, is there any sense in commencing the real action.

Gustav Freitag called this very first introduction into a drama, dealt with above, the "first chord." To carry out the idea one might add that this "first chord" should never enter with a dramatic *fortissimo*, for then all possibility of intensification is cut off. However, this "chord" may be struck as firmly and impressively as the character of the piece permits; but here one point must be insisted on—extreme brevity. Concerning this point you might study, for instance, the beginning of "Lohengrin." The best method is to contrive the opening as a part of the development. Such is the case precisely in "Lohengrin," where the King's address already contains significant details of the plot (the menacing of the realm by foreign foes, the domestic dissension in Brabant, the King's intention to hold a court).

After the "opening chord" there enters (and preferably, in the sung drama, immediately) the *impulsive element*, one might call it the "self-starter." This impulsive element may appear in very various shapes, and, first of all, may be brought into the action either by the "hero" or by his "adversary." To make this point clearer, let us settle in our own minds what we are to understand by the terms *intrigue* and *counter-intrigue* in the drama.

Contrast, antagonism, is the life-blood of the drama. It must present, not persons of similar character, but individuals of most various type, and yet all striving to gain the same end; that is, it must present a conflict, be it serious or playful. The persons (characters) sustaining the drama always divide into two groups of antagonistic aim (intrigue and counter-intrigue), which dominate the dramatic action proper. Thus the action and the grouping of the actors become bipartite, like two hostile camps. Now, all great dramatists observe the elementary rule, not to bestow all the light on one side and all the shadow on the other. A contest between perfect angels and perfect fiends is not only tiresome, monotonous, and absolutely undramatic; it is, besides, untrue to life in a profounder sense. (Shake-speare's "Othello"—*Iago* and *Desdemona*—is only apparently at variance with this rule.) Neither absolutely perfect nor altogether depraved human beings can be found, and it is just the blending of good and evil in each individual that lends a peculiar fascination to his personality. On the stage the sole question is, Which feeling is the more strongly enlisted with regard to a character, our sympathy or our antipathy? A person in whom we dis-cover a bit of ourselves, will always have our sympathy; our antipathy is generally directed against one whose nature differs from ours; we are indifferent towards one who excites neither liking nor dislike. The indifferent character, unhappily a too frequent type in Nature's limitless production, is not available for the drama. Not a single person of the indifferent species should confront us on the stage; even the smallest rôles ought to arouse our sym-pathy or antipathy to some degree. Now let us examine to what extent the characters of the "hero" and the "villain" have the power to thrill us, positively or negatively. One chief rule of the drama is this—to motivate (i.e., to show the incentives for) each person's course of action and the development of his character, either for good or for evil. It must be shown how the likable person gets into difficulties precisely on account of his good qualities (but not how he finds himself accidentally in trouble); on the other hand, some adequate motive (and not necessarily one wholly offensive to the auditor) must be found even for the greatest piece of rascality. Intrigue and counter-intrigue must interest us in equal measure, and each party must be thoroughly justified from its own standpoint in doing what it does in the drama. The pointer of the balance should in due course begin to incline only very gradually toward one side or the other. Again we find a luminous example in "Lohengrin," in which the small number of principals can easily be classified in our scheme. Here the intrigue is unquestionably carried on by Lohengrin and Elsa, the counter-intrigue by Telramund and Ortrud. The King represents the neutral power of exalted justice, that holds sway without respect of persons.

In the beginning of the action the King is precisely as well affected toward Telramund as toward Elsa; only the issue of the ordeal by combat causes him to take Elsa's part decisively. Above all, take note of the fact that Telramund is not the conventional stage-villain, although one may find him played as such on certain mediocre stages. An ingenious device of Wagner's consists in letting

Telramund act in perfect good faith until his death, so that all his actions result from this confidence in his rectitude. The King's significant statement, that he knows Telramund ⸱ to be "the pearl of all virtues," holds good throughout the course of the drama. But it is Telramund's tragic destiny to put blind faith in Ortrud's words, and thus to enmesh himself in wrongdoing. So there can be no doubt that this counter-intrigue even compels our sympathy, and just by this means our interest in the play is intensified. (Only immature youths and flappers are always a-tremble in the theatre for "their" hero or "their" heroine, losing sight of the justifiability for the counter-intrigue.) But even Ortrud is no evildoer of the vulgar stripe. She is the daughter of a princely line, full of ancestral pride, dating back to ancient heathendom, whose very nature revolts against Christendom and a new princely dominion. All her perfidiousness and craftiness, which must surely arouse the auditor's disfavor, serve only the lofty aim of restoring the overthrown altars of her fathers' gods; her defeat is therefore not purely personal, but symbolizes the final downfall of the enchanted realm of heathendom before the almighty power of the Christian Grail; it is the overthrow of the religion of hate by the recognition of forgiving love, by reason of which Ortrud's fall assumes tragic grandeur.

All this really demands a broader treatment in order to show in detail how sharply and positively intrigue and counter-intrigue must be contrasted, and how, although the interest we take in the hero will be the greater, his opponent's character must also be so strongly individualized as not to be at once effaced by impact with the principal personages. Nothing should be made easy for the hero; his victory or defeat must ensue as the final result of the conflict with adversaries worthy of his steel; indeed, the more powerful these adversaries appear, the more stoutly and independently they bear themselves, the more terrible will be the catastrophe for the hero, or the more brilliant his success. This applies equally to the tragic drama and to comedy.

Two possibilities always offer themselves to the poet, and which of these he shall choose depends solely upon the nature of his subject: He may lead off his drama either from the side of the "intrigue" (hero) or from that of the "counter-intrigue" (villain); that is, the exposition may present the position and motives of either of the leading characters first. "Lohengrin" (to cite this instructive example again) unrolls the situation of the hero and heroine before our eyes during the first act;

the part played by their opponents is not effectively presented until the beginning of the second act. The counter-intrigue, chiefly carried on by Ortrud, takes hardly more than a passive part in the larger portion of the first act; it is a characteristic point that Ortrud's participation in the action of Act I is essentially of a pantomimic nature, yet her pantomime must be so speaking that her importance as leader of the counter-intrigue is manifest to every beholder. In "Tristan" and "Walküre," too, the first act is similarly constructed. Reversely, the mirthful action of "Die Meistersinger" advances, after the opening, by way of the counter-intrigue; the first climax (close of Act I) shows Walter apparently defeated, with the counter-intrigue, personified in Beckmesser, triumphant. It is only with the second act that the "intrigue" (carried on by Hans Sachs for Walter and Evchen) begins to set the "villain" at a decided disadvantage. Altogether, the plot of "Die Meistersinger" displays far finer ramifications than that of "Lohengrin," and is therefore deserving of more detailed analysis. For the present our only aim was to elucidate the meaning of "intrigue" and "counter-intrigue," quite apart from the subjective difference between the development of a tragic action and the action of a comedy, whose construction, to be sure, is in many respects subject to the same laws. In general, when a serious subject is in question, that form of construction is more favorable for the hero which presents him at first as taking an active part. "The essence of the drama is conflict and tension; the sooner these are brought into play and carried on by the hero himself, the better." (Freytag.)

To return to the "impulsive element" (which Freytag calls *das erregende Moment*, this being translated by William Archer as "the firing of the fuse," "joining the issue"). For the introduction of the "impulsive element" (a term whose meaning will now be set forth more clearly) two modes are again open to the author's choice: It may be introduced at some moment when the hero arrives at a decision of importance for the subsequent action; or when the "counter-intrigue" commences to take an active part in the development. This impulsive element is one of the most momentous points of the plot; indeed, we may say that an author who fails here to excite and interest his audience, has lost the game. Now, it seems to be demanded by the organization of the dramatic construction that the best way to proceed should be as follows: When the action advances by way of the "intrigue," the impulsive element should be introduced by the "counter-intrigue"; on the other hand, when the "counter-intrigue" carries the action, the hero should introduce the impulsive element. Here we again take contrasting examples from "Lohengrin" and "Meistersinger." In "Lohengrin," whose action is led off by the "intrigue," Telramund introduces the impulsive element, the terrible charge of fratricide against Elsa. In "Die Meistersinger," where the "counter-intrigue" first sets in, the impulsive element is Walter's decision to win Evchen by assuming the rôle of a mastersinger. This decision of Walter's is just as significant for the plot of "Die Meistersinger" as Telramund's charge is for the action of "Lohengrin."

At this point the Exposition, in the narrowest sense of the term, ends; the action has been set in motion, interest is excited, "intrigue" or "counter-intrigue" has pointedly declared itself, and now the conflict can soon begin along a line already established with precision. The real dramatic intensification sets in, and the number of steps required for its consummation depends entirely upon the subject-matter. It follows, that this intensification can comprise several "scenes," whose structure we still have to examine in detail. These scenes must, of course, be so arranged as to contrast with each other and at the same time to so supplement and complete each other as to build up a unified Whole, and so that the interest of the onlooker is excited and held uninterruptedly until the climax and close of the act. And now any other persons actively connected with the main plot, who have not yet been introduced, must be brought forward in a conspicuous manner, excepting when one has in mind to utilize them, for some special heightening of the effect in the second act. In this latter case (recall, for instance, King Marke and Melot in "Tristan," and the Countess in "Figaro") the bearing of such characters on the further action ought here and now to be decisively indicated.

If we do not intend to squeeze the living soul of the drama into chapter and verse (as even Freytag did in his celebrated book), or to classify in categorical succession that which is a living organic complex, we must already consider an important question:

How does one characterize?

In answer to this question I can only enumerate a few of the artifices employed by craftsmen; for the true art of characterization is to be learned from life alone, not with help of any theoretical directions. Anyone who surveys the world with unclouded eye, who has learned not only to watch attentively many varieties of human beings in what they openly do and fail to do, but also to penetrate their secret motives, will gradually acquire the preliminary knowledge needed for sharply outlined characterization. But the drawing of a character in the drama is totally different from that of a personage in a novel. What has to be done in the drama is, to provide, by means of a few concise suggestions, a sketch to which lifelike reality is imparted in mien and gesture through actual presentation by the actor.

Here the chief maxim is, Introduce no subordinate details, however characteristic; only such traits should be emphasized as are of real importance for the progress of the action, that is, for the motives of the persons taking part. From this fundamental rule is derived another—that all features in the original subject-matter which might tend to diminish the dramatic value of a character, should be dropped or modified.

The manner in which a character is introduced is likewise a matter of fundamental importance. On the stage, as in real life, the first impression is decisive. We find it hard to change our opinions, and when a person has once made an impression on us by a strongly sympathetic or antipathetic action, it is extraordinarily difficult for us to change our minds—indeed, it makes us particularly uncomfortable if we are unable to reconcile his later conduct with our first impression. That sudden diversion of the action into a direction not anticipated by the audience, which is one of the dramatist's principal effects, must not be undertaken with respect to the characterization.

Old Aristotle, in his "Poetics," already stated the eternal dramaturgic truth that the Action should be the first and chiefest matter, the Persons taking second place. This does not mean, of course, that the drawing of the characters should be neglected. On the contrary, it is of extraordinary importance for the finer ramifications of the action that their motivation should proceed from the characters themselves. To carry out the architectonic simile we might say that the action is the mere shell of the house, while the characterization displays its interior arrangement. But one must first have the house ready in all its parts before one can habitably arrange it for the "persons," although one must naturally take into consideration, even in the rough draught, the individual requirements of the several inhabiting personalities. The mutual relations between characters and action can nowhere be more instructively studied than by a comparison of the sketches for "Die

Meistersinger" with the finished poem. We shall then speedily comprehend a clever and pointed observation of Diderot's in a dramaturgic essay: The plan of a drama can be made, and even well made, before the author knows anything about the character with which he is to endow his personages. Human beings of very diverse character are always exposed to the same casualties. One who sacrifices his daughter may be ambitious, weak, or obstinate; one who is alarmed for his sweetheart may be a philistine or a hero, tender or jealous, prince or servant. The characters will be well chosen when the situations are made more difficult or exciting by the choice.

Out of the endless variety of human characters the Art of Drama very early selected certain types which, with some more or less considerable modifications, continually reappear in the end at all periods and among all peoples. It smacks of the mechanical and conventional when we hear an actor or singer everlastingly talking about his or her "specialty"; and yet the mere term "specialty" does not necessarily lead to a mere swapping of shop talk. Any actor, however versatile he may be, after all possesses certain advantages or disadvantages in voice, appearance and age, which confine him within positive limits. And this being the case in the spoken drama,

in opera the "specialties" will be still more
strictly limited, as singing voices are more
sharply differentiated than speaking voices.
So, if we would not sacrifice one of the most
characteristic and beautiful peculiarities of the
musical drama, the ensemble, to a theoretical
delusion to which Wagner himself had not by
any means always subscribed in practice, the
librettist must be fairly well informed as to
how his rôles are to be distributed among the
various classes of voice and of specialty actors.
As a practical example, take the well-considered
voice-distribution in "Die Meistersinger,"
whose musical crowning-point is presented
by the famous quintet. The usual dramatic
rôles (without taking account of intermediate
and farcical parts in detail) may be divided into
the following basic classes, in which the principal contrasts among humankind (man and
woman, young and old, high and low, heroic
and ignominious, serious and merry, good and
bad) are likewise included.

Hero, Heroine (Leading man, Leading
woman).
Heavy father, Heavy mother (Leading old
man, Leading old woman). (Heavy villain,
Heavy lead).
Elderly comedian, Elderly comédienne
(First light or low com.).

Elderly lover (either sex).
Light juvenile comedian, comédienne.
Excentric comedian, Chambermaid (Bonvivant, Soubrette).
Second low comedian, Ingénue.

In the opera we specify, according to class of voice or character:

Soprano: dramatic and juvenile dramatic, coloratura, soubrette.
Mezzo-soprano: serious or comic.
Alto: serious or comic.
Tenor: heroic, lyric, buffo.
Baritone: serious or comic.
Bass: serious or comic.

Now, it is not quite so simple as one is apt to think, to unite these acting rôles with singing rôles in such a way that a really satisfactory combination results. For modern operas are—I am tempted to say, unfortunately —no longer, as they still were in Italy at Rossini's time, written to order for some particular ensemble which the composer had opportunity to study during his work. Nowadays operas are mostly composed, as it were, at random, without knowing (except in the case of a few favored instances) in the least where or by whom they will first be performed. This is like planning a house without knowing where it is to be built or who will live in it. In view of this drawback one cannot be too urgently advised to adhere as closely as may be to traditional rôles (types), for that is the only way in which an author can insure his work against an absolutely perverted and inadequate performance. To one who prefers the concrete to the abstract I would offer this good advice: If you live in a place where there is a halfway efficient opera, keep the members of the company in view as you work; always imagine—even if you do not mean to have your opera given there—how one singer or another, who most nearly approaches some type of your fancy, would sing or act that particular part; this will save you from the worst mistakes. And, more especially, observe whether a theatre of average size is in a position to furnish capable players for the rôles your work requires, viewed as one in the regular repertory. (These remarks are not intended for people who expect to have *Festspielhäuser* erected for their particular benefit; neither geniuses nor megalomaniacs will have any use for them.) Just here many a beginner has blundered, to his everlasting hurt. It is self-evident, in consideration of the rarity of fine, big tenor voices and of the huge re-muneration which their lucky possessors receive, that composers have to be sparing in their use of such expensive material. Besides, one big tenor rôle, either heroic or lyric, is quite sufficient; alongside of this, excepting for a few very small parts, only a tenor buffo will usually be available. Study and admire Wagner's practical economy in this matter.— Of course, the class of voice you choose must be in correspondence with the character of the hero, who will in all probability be a tenor or a baritone—very seldom a bass. For a radiant hero (Tannhäuser, Lohengrin, Siegfried, Tristan, Parsifal, etc.) the choice will always fall on an heroic tenor; a dæmonic hero will be represented by a baritone (Don Juan, the Dutchman, etc.). For a jovial hero (Figaro) a light baritone is preferable to a tenor on account of its greater flexibility. To the heroic tenor the dramatic soprano is the counterpart; to the lyric tenor, the juvenile dramatic soprano; to the baritone buffo or the tenor buffo, the soubrette. Somewhat outside our modern classification stands the coloratura soprano, to whom, in modern operas, hardly any rôles except parodistic ones are likely to be given. And even such rôles are conditioned on the composer's ability to write coloratura parts—something one cannot say for Richard Strauss as regards his Zerbinetta. Touching the identity of the serious bass with the "heavy father," of the bass buffo with the elderly "light comedian," no words need be wasted. The alto voice is similarly limited, in general, to the characterization of elderly "heavy" or "light" comédiennes; seeing that really fine alto voices are growingly scarce, one often does better to employ a mezzo-soprano. You will do well, after sketching your plan, to notice how the principal personages are contrasted in the principal ensemble scenes, as regards vocal quality. We know that Meyerbeer used to make his librettist transpose and remodel entire scenes when this association of the voices did not suit him at all points. It is true that modern dramatic taste no longer permits that a character should enter merely and evidently to participate in an ensemble; but when the entrance of some valuable voice can be cleverly motivated, the stage-effect is assuredly heightened by bringing on one's best troops in full strength at the proper moment. And the singers, too (as Lortzing points out in the conversation cited above), want *effective rôles* above all things, and none of them cares to sit by himself in his dressing-room while his colleagues are singing a popular ensemble. In this particular Wagner learned more from Meyerbeer and Scribe than he liked to acknowledge; only he did not cast his characters for external effect, but for essentially dramatic ends. Special care should be taken to give the principal singers proper intervals of rest—a point too often lost sight of. Some acts in opera are so unskillfully arranged that the hero cannot leave the stage for a moment; and, being on the stage, he must be occupied to fit the situation. Therefore, take care that he has a chance to vanish from the scene at one time or another. Wagner brought this about very neatly in the first and second acts of "Siegfried," although both rely almost entirely on the leading rôle. In such cases, of course, an interesting situation must immediately follow the hero's disappearance. Beginners often motivate a principal's exit so naïvely that the effect cannot be otherwise than unintentionally comical. You should test your work to see if the requirements of the actor are satisfied, these being "good rôles, strong effects, sparing the singer's strength, convenient arrangement of the scenes." And now, first of all, let us establish precisely what is meant by a "scene," and how it is constructed.

Within the Act, whose beginning and end are clearly marked by the rise and fall of the curtain, there is felt a necessity for subdivisions, both because of technical considerations (stage-management) and with regard to intrinsic poetical needs.

The Scene is a miniature reflection of the Act, and is founded on almost the same laws of construction as the latter. Thus, in the scene, Exposition, Suspense, and Dénouement, the three principal elements, also play a decisive part. In so far, the spoken drama corresponds with the sung drama. But now there appears an important difference between these two branches of art: Whereas the spoken drama permits of only the aforesaid subdivisions, which are derived from the very nature of the drama, in the earlier "opera," which operated solely with finished musical "numbers," there was the possibility of subdividing the act according to the individual pieces of music. Out of this grew the "opera in numbers," in which the composer no longer had to set to music organic parts of a dramatic whole, but simply "numbers," i.e., highly effective pieces of music without inner connection, which were frequently even interpolated as afterthoughts anywhere in some very loosely-contrived plot—much as is often done nowadays in the case of operettas. Where such a piece of music stood, whether in the beginning, middle or end of the play, often made no difference, and even the succession of these interpolated pieces would be changed higgledy-piggledy, so that it frequently happened that the pieces were given to other persons in the drama than those for whom they were originally intended. It was Richard Wagner, as we know, who finally put an end to this abuse with his "Tannhäuser"; for Wagner's earlier works, not excepting "The Flying Dutchman," which is generally lauded as opening the new era, still display the old division into numbers, as the scores distinctly show. In after-years, to be sure, Wagner tried to camouflage this state of affairs by presenting (in his "Gesammelte Schriften und Dichtungen") the poems of both "Rienzi" and "The Flying Dutchman" divided according to "scenes," so as to make it appear as if he had grouped these earlier poems with a view to scenic subdivision, and not from a purely musical standpoint. And it must be admitted that the "scenes" of the later reading outwardly match the earlier "numbers" exactly; but on more careful examination one sees that the inner construction corresponds rather with the musical grouping attached to the score than with the new dramatic disposition. At all events, the fact that the old musical terminology could here so easily be converted into scenic paraphrase proves how far Wagner's creative consciousness had already turned toward the logical division into scenes while he was outwardly as yet in bondage to the old order in numbers. This becomes even clearer in "Tannhäuser." Here we still see a veiled glimmer of the "number" style (Elisabeth's entrance aria, Wolfram's romance, the building-up of the finales), but the purely dramatic construction of the poem has advanced so far that the Acts are no longer divided from a musical, but from a dramatic, viewpoint. Thus the first act logically divides into four scenes, the second also into four, the third into three, each of which forms in itself a complete musico-dramatic Whole. Herewith we have arrived at an important stage; henceforward musical and dramatic groupings coincide; the "number" no longer stands contrasted with the "scene," for the scene becomes, so to say, a number. And so that old difficulty is removed which is noticeable, at least on the surface, even in "The Marriage of Figaro." Mozart's librettist had made the attempt, never again repeated, to subdivide his book not only according to vocal numbers, but also according to dramatic scenes. Thereupon arose a distinct discrepancy between the dramatic and musical groupings. For example, the first act contained eight scenes, but nine numbers (within the numbers the scene frequently changes, and within the scenes the number!). To this is added the inconvenience, that the numbers run consecutively through the whole opera, whereas the numbering of the scenes naturally begins anew with each act. It is evident that, in contrast with this confusion, Wagner's terminology from "Tannhäuser" onward presents the greatest advantages.

In principle, however, Mozart solved in "Figaro" the problem of the musical drama quite as completely as Wagner. For Mozart already recognized the importance of tonality for dramatic expression, and thereby endowed long passages of the drama with a well-rounded unity such as, apart from Weber, it was left for the zeal of the creator of "Tannhäuser" to rediscover. This is not, of course, the place for a detailed analysis of these intimate relations between book and music; yet it must be plain that a good libretto cannot be planned without taking certain tonal effects into consideration. True enough, such a course is more a matter of instinct than of intellectual calculation; but surely one may say: If the book is, dramatically, well and consistently constructed, the composer, on his part, will find the right path. Personally, at least, I have found that a dramatic "turning-around-in-a-circle" always finds its musical analogue, and that, once any *dramatic* redundance was recognized, it was always surprisingly easy to effect the necessary *musical* reduction, or "cut." As a composer, too, I had involuntarily turned about in a modulatory circle and had returned to the key in which I started at the beginning of the "redundance." I find this wholly personal experience corroborated in an article by Weingartner, "Striche bei Wagner" [Cuts in Wagner]: "Wherever a poetical transition is feasible, a musical transition also results with inexplicable ease." \

Contrast of effect is an important matter for consideration, especially with reference to the musical construction. Not only the separate acts, but also the scenes in their mutual relations, must exhibit the necessary contrasts. For this point the first act of "Tannhäuser" (in the earlier version) affords instructive examples. It consists of four scenes:

1. The Venusberg.
2. Venus and Tannhäuser.
3. Tannhäuser. A young Shepherd. Pilgrims.
4. Tannhäuser. The Landgrave and the Singers.

The four scenes of this act match each other pairwise in a species of parallel construction which Wagner, in particular, carried to extreme perfection. The first scene both corresponds and contrasts with the third, and the second scene with the fourth. Between the second and third scenes there lies, outwardly marked by the mere lightning-like change of scene, an amazing, stupendous contrast. Here, the sultry atmosphere of the "grottoes of bliss"; there, the reanimating breath of new-born Springtide, combined (what an exquisite touch!) on the one hand with the activities of "Frau Venus," the goddess of love, set off against "Frau Holda," the bounteous dispenser of Spring's gifts. The first and third scenes are devoted to setting forth these opposites, the first exclusively as a dance-scene, the third likewise a purely pantomimic scene, at least for Tannhäuser himself, confronted with whom the figures of the Shepherd and the Pilgrims are mere *staffage* enhancing the illusion. The real action therefore is strictly confined to the second and fourth scenes, whose upshot we can briefly indicate as follows:

Scene 2.   Desertion of Venus.
Scene 4.   Return to Elisabeth.

In these we again note the sharpest contrast. Venus and Elisabeth personify "amor" and "charitas"; love as enjoyment is Venus's domain, love as pity that of Elisabeth. That both conceptions of love are equally justifiable, so that Venus is not set below Elisabeth, but on an equality with her, was emphasized sharply enough by Wagner, who defended himself against the implication that his "Tannhäuser" revealed a "tendency toward specifically Christian, impotent pietism." ("Eine Mittheilung an meine Freunde.") So it came that Wagner in later years even gave a further development to the character of Venus, in the so-called Paris version: "My characterization of Venus was stiff; some few good features, but no genuine life. Here I have added quite a number of verses; the goddess of ecstasy really becomes moving, and Tannhäuser's agony grows real, so that his cry to Maria bursts from his soul like an outcry of profound dismay." Here we shall not attempt a disquisition on the value or valuelessness of the Paris revision. We shall only point out that dramatically—especially in the economy of the scenic arrangement—the first act, which originally was divided into two balanced sections, lost that balance in the later version, with the result that the overextended first half undeniably impairs our impressionability for the charm of the second part. But note one important point: As to the first half of Act I, Wagner characterized this entire section as simply one tremendous intensification of effect up to the decisive outcry, "Maria!" And this "Maria!" ought to burst forth with such poignant energy, that "from it flows swift apprehension of the instantly following marvellous disencharming of the Venusberg, and of the translocation to the home-valley, as the necessary fulfilment of an imperative demand by a heart driven to desperate decision." Surely, there are but few situations in the dramatic literature of all periods and peoples, that may be compared with this thrilling moment in "Tannhäuser." Let us examine, exclusively from the standpoint of dramatic construction, how Wagner prepares this moment, and how he builds up the second scene in the first act. The very first gesture in this scene clearly reveals the situation at the beginning—Tannhäuser raises his head convulsively, as if starting up out of a dream; Venus caressingly draws him back. This brings before our eyes the most vital contrast within the scene—the discontent of Tannhäuser, sated with the pleasures of the Venusberg, and the still unwavering love of the goddess, who will not for the world allow her favorite knight to depart. From this opposition of wills arises the conflict of the scene and its final result: Tannhäuser's will wins the day, but the curse of the goddess pursues him and never lets him find peace. (We have to admit that we do not divine the effectiveness of the goddess's curse until the opening of the second act, where the menacing Motive of the Curse intrudes like a spectre into the joyous orchestral prelude.) Between beginning and end are all stages of transition, and it is quite in keeping with dramatic truth that it seems at moments (for heightening the suspense) as if Tannhäuser had renounced his purpose and yielded to the desire of the goddess. This always appears in the first half of his praise-song, but in the second half of the song he as regularly returns to his longing for freedom. Within the scene its division into grand intensifications is clearly marked by the triple repetition of the praise-song (raised by a semitone each time, be it noted), in which, after celebrating the goddess, Tannhäuser vents his longing for liberty with ever-increasing vehemence. Now, it is most instructive, dramatically, to observe how Venus reacts each time. Before the first strophe of the song she does not take Tannhäuser's plaints all too tragically. She replies to him with a couple of trifling phrases in the tone of an aggrieved coquette, ending with an appeal to sing the praises of love and the goddess of love. Then follows the first strophe of the song, whose close always runs: "Aus deinem Reiche muss ich fliehn, o Königin, Göttin, lass mich ziehn!" (From thy domain I must flee: O queen, goddess, let me go!) Whereas Tannhäuser before had only mourn-

fully asked: "Shall I ne'er ·hear them, never
see them more?" we now hear for the first
time his firm decision to abandon Venus for
ever. Accordingly, she answers in a more
serious tone, yet still thinking she has to do
with a mere momentary whim, a fit of de-
pression; she coaxes him much as a mother
coaxes her spoiled darling, and questions
herself: "Wherein was my love remiss?"
Tannhäuser responds with yet more glowing
praise of the goddess of love—but also with
still more vehement desire for freedom. Thereupon Venus starts up passionately, wounded
in her profoundest affections, and hurls at him
the reproach:

> Thou darest to scorn my love?
> Thou praisest it, and still wouldst flee from it?
> My charm has now grown wearisome to thee?

With fine feminine instinct Venus has found
the true reason for his enigmatic attitude, although she is mistaken in supposing that
Tannhäuser "scorns" her, for it is only the
war of emotions that drives him to his strangely
contradictory behavior. And for a moment
he attempts to pacify the goddess, calling her
"lovely," and declaring the very excess of her
charms to be the reason that he must go—
supposedly a sort of "compliment" for Venus.
She, however, is not deceived by mere phrases
born of embarrassment. While calling him

a traitor, hypocrite; thankless wretch, she none the less reveals in the same breath, in truly feminine fashion, that she will not let him go. But now, when Tannhäuser warmly and openly avows:

> Ne'er was my manhood fuller, never truer,
> Than now, when I must part from thee forever!

she changes her tone. She knows that an unfaithful man is more effectively controlled by loving allurement than by reproaches, and of the former she is past-mistress. At her beck is disclosed the blissful grotto:

> A feast of joy shall celebrate our union,
> In our rejoicing let love's rites be crowned!
> Bring thou to love no timid sacrifice—
> Nay! with love's goddess taste the ecstasy of bliss.

From afar sounds the seductive song of the Sirens, and it seems as though Tannhäuser, lost in blissful fascination, were unable to carry out his determination to depart. Venus herself, gently urging him on, asks half-jestingly, half-seductively, "My knight, my lover, wilt thou go?" And he, in bewildering enravishment, sweeps his harpstrings with ecstatic mien and for the third time sings the praise of Venus's charms. And Venus, like the uninitiate beholder, feels no doubt that this time, intoxicated by love's allurements, Tannhäuser will finally forfeit his freedom to the goddess. And yet—take note of the tremendous dramatic revulsion—in the second half of the praise-song Tannhäuser once more intones his longing for liberty; so steadfast is his will that only for a moment can it be made to waver, but remains unbroken. For the third time he implores the goddess, "Let me go!" And at this juncture Venus's demeanor likewise changes; till now only the loving woman, she reveals herself as the haughty, ireful goddess. Prophetically she foresees Tannhäuser's wretchedness out in "the world": "What thou desirest, be thy lot! Depart!" She feels that sometime he will return, remorseful and broken. Tannhäuser's pride hurls back the defiance: "Ne'er shall I return to thee!" Thereupon—again how wonderful a contrast!—the goddess, but now so majestical, once more becomes the loving woman that sees herself bereft of her last hope ("Ha! shouldst thou ne'er return to me"), and therefore in utmost desperation launches a curse upon the whole world—none of humankind shall enjoy love, if the goddess of love herself must sigh in vain. And now comes the grand intensification; Venus plays her last trump:

VENUS:—O come, come back to me again!
TANNHÄUSER:—No more may me love's joy delight!
VENUS:—Come back, whene'er thy heart shall plead!

[85]

TANNH.:—Thy lover leaves thee now for aye!
VENUS:—And if they all should spurn thee forth?
TANNH.:—Repentance lifts the curse from me.
VENUS:—Forgiveness ne'er shall make thee whole!
        Return, when naught can save thy soul!
TANNH.—My soul—my soul confides in Mary!

(Venus cowers to earth with a cry, and vanishes. The scene changes with lightning-like swiftness.)

Observe how in this intensification—so brief in point of time, so overwhelming in effect —all the elements in the subsequent development of the Tannhäuser drama are already anticipated:

"And if they all should spurn thee forth" (Act II).

"Repentance lifts the curse from me" (Act II, close).

"Forgiveness ne'er shall make thee whole" (T.'s pilgrimage).

"My soul confides in Mary" (Elisabeth's pleading, and martyr-death, in Act III).

One can admire the genius of the youthful Wagner, who here intuitively found the right path, only the more unreservedly when one notes how the later Wagner played the mischief, dramatically, with his own creation in the Paris version. As Wagner remarked to Röckel: "But how little can the artist expect to see his own intention fully reproduced in

any interpretation, when he himself is confronted by his art-work as by an enigma,
concerning which he may be as readily deceived as others!" Compare with the above
quotation the following version[1] of the same
situation:

> VENUS:—Come back to me! Believe me,
>   My fondest love thou'lt find!
> TANNHÄUSER:—Goddess, whoe'er doth leave thee,
>   Leaves love for aye behind.
> VENUS:—Resist no longing proudly
>   That leads thee back to me!
> TANNH.:—My longing is for battle;
>   I seek no bliss, no joys,
>   O Goddess, mark me rightly,
>   'Tis death alone I prize!
> VENUS:—If even Death avoid thee,
>   Were there no grave for thee!
> TANNH.:—My heart shall find thro' penance
>   Its death and grave in peace.
> VENUS:—Peace ne'er shall be thy portion,
>   Nor safety for thy soul!
>   Come back to me and rest thee,
>   My love shall make thee whole!
> TANNH.:—Goddess of rapture, not in thee—
>   For peace my soul trusteth in Mary!
>
>   (*Terrible crash. Venus vanishes.*)

[1]As given in the "Gesammelte Schriften und Dichtungen,"
this being the real poetic version; for actual performance
according to the Paris version, there is used a poor retransla-
tion of the French text to which Wagner wrote the music.

At all events, this comparison of the two versions is worthy of note if only because it shows how a master of the drama sought a similar intensification of the same scene, at different periods, through the employment of different means.

The outcry, "My soul confides in Mary!" unquestionably marks the external climax of the first act; and yet, in the course of this same act, it is surpassed by one still more profoundly moving. "Elisabeth" is the magic word that marks the climax of the second half of the act. "Zu ihr! zu ihr!" sounds not at all like the distressful cry "Maria!" Now Tannhäuser's heart beats high "in süssem, ungestümen Drängen," and the gay notes of the hunting-horns are but an echo from the hero's own breast. It is worth while to follow out in detail how this simpler fourth scene of Act I is worked up to a climax in like fashion to the second scene. With respect to the dramatico-musical significance of the scenic construction following the completed "Tannhäuser" and the completed "Lohengrin," through which he first fully realized the tendency toward which subconscious instinct had urged him, Wagner left us the clearest explanation:

"As the framing of my scenes excluded all foreign and superfluous details, and con-

centrated interest upon the prevailing mood,
similarly the entire structure of my drama
was built up into a definite unity, whose easily
recognizable members were fashioned out of
precisely those fewer scenes or situations that
were in regular course decisive for the mood.
In none of these scenes was any mood allowed
to develop which did not stand in significant
relation to the moods of the other scenes, so
that the development of moods from scene
to scene and the obvious concatenation of
this development constituted precisely the
unifying element in the expression of the dramatic action. Each of these leading moods,
from the very nature of the subject, had to
find its individual musical expression, which
materialized to the sense of hearing as a
definite musical theme. And as, in the course
of the drama, the contemplated amplification
of one decisive principal mood could be produced only by keeping before the mental
vision the continuing development of moods
from scene to scene, it necessarily followed
that the musical expression, as the immediate
factor in determining the sensuous emotion,
must decisively participate in bringing this
development to its highest intensity. And
this was brought about quite naturally by a
continuous characteristic interweaving of the
leading-motives, extending, not merely over

one scene (as earlier in the separate operatic vocal numbers), but over the entire drama, and throughout in most intimate relation to the poetic intention [characterization]."

In order to analyze the construction of a Wagner Act more in detail, and at the same time to explain the nature of the Exposition and the Intensification, we shall—following our study of a Wagner Scene in "Tann-häuser"—do best to take up the first act of "Lohengrin," which may be considered as the first really mature product of the music-dramatist Wagner, and one which, compared with his later works, possesses the advantages of simplicity and lucidity. Just from this work, where—in contrast to "Tannhäuser"— Exposition and Action proceed in unity along the same line, we can learn many *practical* details for the plan of construction which Wagner, in the remarks above quoted, could only suggest *theoretically*. Referring to "Lohengrin," Wagner declared that his principal aim was "extreme clearness of presentation," and this clarity is displayed more especially in the wonderfully simple dramatic framework of the opera.

The characters of the Lohengrin drama can readily be classified as parties of the "intrigue" or the "counter-intrigue." Strictly speaking, the action of the drama is carried on by only two persons, Elsa and Ortrud. From Ortrud issues the fearful charge of fratricide; she is also the promotor of the catastrophe in the second and third acts; and finally succeeds in so deluding the guileless Elsa that the latter all but makes common cause with Ortrud. Telramund is merely Ortrud's tool; and even Lohengrin, although nominally the hero of the drama, is in reality—from a dramatico-technical viewpoint—only the loftiest expression of Elsa's purity, because of which she is held worthy of the Grail's protection as personified in Lohengrin. Thus Lohengrin is, in a manner of speaking, only the personification of aid against an unjust accusation. Of course, the drama as played on the stage shows Lohengrin and Elsa in visible contention with Telramund and Ortrud; hence, the defeat of Telramund in Act I also comprehends Elsa's victory and Ortrud's failure. The pointer of the balance is King Heinrich, enthroned above the parties as court of last resort. The "Heerrufer" (Herald) is nothing but a subordinate assistant of the King's, a sort of living official "State Gazette," and the youthful Count Gottfried, on whose fate turn both the opening and the close of the drama, is reduced to a lay-figure. With the exception of the young Count, Wagner already introduces all his personages in the first act;—but observe how differently they are brought on. At the very opening there are on the stage, besides the chorus, the King, the Herald, Telramund and Ortrud. Now, it is a most important point that Wagner, while bringing on all his leading characters in the first act, leaves one of them, Ortrud, the chief person in the "counter-intrigue," comparatively inactive, reducing her part to but little more than dumb-show. Only in the final ensemble does Ortrud have a few, not specially important, words, and even these are quite lost in the closing jubilation. For the rest, the onlooker is left to suppose that she is the motive power behind Telramund's accusation; but this does not become a certainty until the second act. It was a masterstroke of Wagner's to defer the exposition of this character, Ortrud, to the beginning of the second act, and under the shroud of darkness; and this exposition, in its musical tonality (the gloomy F-sharp minor, the relative of the Lohengrin key of A major), stands in equally sharp contrast to the first act. The characterization of Ortrud being thus saved up for Act II, the style and method in which Wagner introduces the remaining personages of the drama in the course of Act I becomes all the more instructive. This act embraces only three scenes, and of these scenes each

has its "hero"—Telramund, Elsa, Lohengrin.
The dramatic intensification in these scenes
may be summed up in the phrases Accusation,
Sore Need of the Helpless Defendant, Advent
of the Deliverer, Victory of the Righteous
Cause. The first scene is the Scene of Suspense, the second a Scene of Intensification,
the third the Dénouement. This first act is,
in a way, a drama within the drama, rounded
off and finished—all but Lohengrin's "Ne'er
shalt thou ask me!" that arouses forebodings
of possible further conflict. But this merely
by the way. I designated Scene I as that of
Telramund, although King Heinrich opens
it with a broad exposition. However, as
I have already pointed out, this *exposé* of
the King's possesses.only general introductory
significance. True, Wagner utilizes this speech
for a characterization of the King, but a
stronger dramatic interest sets in only with
the words of Telramund, whom the King has
just praised as a "pearl of virtue," and whose
accusation must, therefore, go far to carry
conviction to the minds of the men-at-arms
and—*nota bene!*—of the audience, as well.
A very skillful little trick of exposition
lies in the point that, while Telramund
alone actually carries the action, there is
in his speech an allusion to Ortrud, whom
he introduces to the King in a significant

manner. Telramund follows up the charge of fratricide by the not less weighty accusation of a secret love-intrigue with an unknown knight. In eager suspense we await the woman so grievously aspersed, and the solemn ceremonial which marks the proceedings of the King, the men-at-arms, and the Herald, yet further heightens the tension of the beholders. For the fact that Wagner imposes silence here upon Ortrud there is still another reason; the color of this first scene is wholly masculine, it bristles with weapons, it is a tribunal of men. Now follows the entrance of the womanly element, and Elsa's appearance in simple garb, clad in the color of innocence, immediately impresses the onlookers in her favor—particularly against the musical background—so that Telramund's terrible accusations count for nothing from that moment. We feel that this maiden cannot be guilty of the crimes imputed to her; Telramund may indeed be a man of honor, but there must be something wrong with the case. Such is the idea that everyone in the audience, from highest to lowest, gets intuitively, not by reasoning; and this is just the effect the dramatist wants. He would have us take sides, but only sympathetically, not combatively; and from the moment of her entrance we sympathize with Elsa. Our sympathy is increased by her modest demeanor, her waiving defense, and her first sorrowful words: "My poor brother!" So complete an impression of touching helplessness! But Elsa is not so helpless, after all, as her enemies fancy; in impassioned prayer she has had a vision— to her aid came a glorious knight clad all in shining armor, and he it is whom she chooses for her defender. Now, too, the King and the men-at-arms doubt no longer—Elsa is guiltless. "Friedrich, thou honorable màn, bethink thee well whom thou accusest!"— so the King exhorts Telramund, whose good faith he cannot yet bring himself to question. But Telramund accepts Elsa's avowal simply as a proof of her guilt; he is a rough warrior, little used to argument; the sword alone defends his honor; hence his knightly challenge to whomsoever will enter the lists with him for Elsa. But no man of Brabant will venture. Even the King's power has reached its limit —God alone can decide the issue. Telramund solemnly vows to sustain his charge at the hazard of his life. Elsa also confides her fate to the hand of God—the unknown, glorious knight shall be her defender. In reward she offers him her heart, her hand, and her crown. Anxious suspense—will the knight appear? First call to combat—he appears not. Telramund already triumphs. Second signal—

long, anxious silence. "In lowering silence God hath judged!" say all the men. No doubt remains—Elsa is doomed. And now mark well how, from this profoundest depth, there develops a tremendous, unheard-of revulsion of feeling. To this Elsa's final prayer leads up musically (out of gloomy A-flat minor into radiant A major) and dramatically ("As I beheld him, let him come!"). Scarcely are these words sung, when the first ecstatic exclamation of the tenors resounds: "Look! look! how strange a marvel!" Imposing is the dramatic tableau at Lohengrin's advent, where the animated individualizing of the chorus, free from all conventionality, is striking. It is a superb feature that the whole jubilant movement emanates from the crowd, whereas the principals, though remaining in the foreground, express through their individual poses their attitude toward the knight's approach. The King, as beseems his knighthood, overlooks the scene from his point of vantage; Telramund and Ortrud are, at first, petrified by dread and astonishment; Elsa, who with mounting ecstasy has listened to the cries of the men without venturing at the outset to turn round, at the last moment exclaims aloud on catching sight of Lohengrin. Telramund gazes on Lohengrin in speechless amazement, while Ortrud, who hitherto has maintained her cold, haughty bearing, is convulsed by mortal fear on view of the swan. We have reached the climax of the act; the deliverer has come, and his resplendent figure gives promise of victory for the right. The knights hail him as one sent by God. We now follow with lively interest the hero's every act; first, his farewell to the swan, behind which, as Ortrud's panic betrays, there lies a mystery (the swan is the youthful count, spellbound by Ortrud); then Lohengrin's prophetic greeting of the King, and lastly the unerring certanty with which he addresses Elsa, never seen till then. But Lohengrin may not support the princess unconditionally—and on this point hinges the entire drama; twice, with all solemnity, he forbids her to question him (the "Frageverbot"), and Elsa passes judgment on herself by the admission: "What doubt could ever guiltier be than doubt that slew my trust in thee?" We must recognize that the "Frageverbot" is no mere passing "effect," but an essential link in the action. Lohengrin, now no longer the semi-divinity, but only the enraptured man, thereupon raises Elsa with the avowal of his love. Confronting Telramund, he roundly asserts Elsa's innocence, and even the count's supporters warn him not to engage in combat with the heaven-sent champion. But Telramund, as a man of his word, will "rather die than live a coward," and violently asseverates that Lohengrin is a sorcerer. Thus the ordeal by combat is the sole remaining resort, and its ceremonial preparation is accompanied by prayers. Once more intensest suspense, as the fight sways for a time undecided, till at last Lohengrin strikes down the count with a sweeping blow. All expect Lohengrin to despatch his adversary, but he grants him his forfeit life that he may atone his guilt through repentance. This, like the "Frageverbot," is another incident bearing the germ of further conflict. The following outbreak of jubilation, in which all but Telramund and Ortrud join, forms a brilliant close to the admirably constructed act.

The "intrigue" has conquered; the "bearers of the counter-intrigue" are apparently stricken powerless to earth;—but (and this is genuine drama) it only *appears* so, for they are not. If they were so in fact, the drama would be at an end both as regards outward show and inward essence. The continuation of the visible action depends on the question, What will Friedrich and Ortrud do now? The course of the spiritual action is influenced by the conflicts into which Elsa is drawn by Lohengrin's prohibition. The question as to the whereabouts of the young count, which furnished the motive for the first conflict, now seems to be finally dismissed, and is not settled until the very end of the drama, when hardly anybody still bears it in mind. So the leading question of the drama is no longer, Where is the young count?—however important this may be in itself—but, Will Elsa keep her promise? Further analysis of this dramatic development may be carried out by the ambitious student along similar lines. For the interest of the apprentice in the business of the master is, after all, the final preparation for masterpieces of his own.

CHAPTER IV

A Practical Example

Eugène Scribe's Libretto-Technic
Illustrated by the Book of the Comedy-Opera
"Le Part du Diable"

Eugène Scribe (born in Paris, Dec. 24, 1791, died there Feb. 20, 1861) was indubitably one of the cleverest and technically most skillful dramaturgists who ever lived, and, more particularly, remains unrivalled as an author of comedies (his *chef d'œuvre* in this branch is "Le Verre d'eau"). The art of tying most intricate knots and loosing them with equal ingenuity—that art in which Beaumarchais, with respect to comedy, was probably the first to excel, though not in so high a degree— was developed by Scribe into a never-failing, brilliant technic. Even if he later applied himself to wholesale production in company with numerous collaborators, his best works will nevertheless long remain in full vigor on the stage, because, however little of real life they may reflect, their construction is perfect from the point of stage-effect, so that they never fail when adequately interpreted. Scribe also marks an epoch in the history of the opera-libretto, and it is significant that nearly all the great Parisian operatic successes in the first half of the nineteenth century were won with books by Scribe. Most famous of all was his connection with Meyerbeer, who worried him by alterations in his books from the composer's standpoint, and therefore had only himself to thank that most of the librettos he had from Scribe were so absurdly constructed. Only the book of "The Huguenots" is a partial exception to this rule. What Scribe could achieve in the domain of serious opera, he showed in his remarkable books for Auber's "La Muette de Portici" and Halévy's "La Juive," two masterpieces greatly admired by Wagner. Still more characteristic of Scribe's originality are his comedy-opera librettos, especially those written for Auber, whose temper was most congenial to the spirit of Scribe's comedies. "Le Domino noir," "Fra Diavolo" and "Le Part du Diable" are the best librettos of this kind, and combine humor very effectively with romance, like "La Dame blanche" written for Boieldieu. In particular, the book for "Le Part du Diable," produced soon after "Le Verre d'eau," during Scribe's best period, displays an inventive power and technic fully on a level with that comedy—indeed, vividly reminds one of it by various traits and artistic devices. For detailed description of Scribe's manner of working I shall avail myself of the disclosures made by Ernest Legouvé, one of the best and most successful among Scribe's collaborators, in an almost unknown little "Conférence" (lecture), which he afterwards had printed (Paris, 1874). This booklet of barely fifty pages contains a real compendium of practical experiences, and is therefore deserving of careful examination. Legouvé speaks of the five essential points in Scribe's dramatic work, enumerating them as follows:

1. Invention of the Subject-matter.
2. The Plot.
3. The Characters.
4. The Style.
5. The Stage-directions.

Legouvé writes delightfully about Scribe's inexhaustible talent for invention, which turned everything it touched into stage-plays; he was, after a fashion, a "dramatic Don Juan," making love to every lovely idea until he had enjoyed it, and then casting it aside for a new one. He wrote four hundred plays, but improvised at least four thousand, sketching them and forgetting them. Everything nourished his inventive powers—an incident while out walking, a conversation, reading, a visit. His scenic fancy was ever at work. Hardly had he discovered a subject, than he began the elaboration of the plot. No other than Racine had already remarked, "When my plot is settled, my piece is written"; and Lessing opined, "Not mere imagination, but *practical* imagination, gives proof of the creative mind."

At the very inception of the work, Scribe would sketch out the entire scenario. Legouvé narrates that Scribe, when the situations of the drama "Adrienne Lecouvreur," which they had been discussing together, were scarcely settled, precisely fixed the successive entrances, and, with unerring certainty, grouped the personages of the first act in the very manner in which they finally remained. The subsequent elaboration merely emphasized the rapidity with which Scribe had planned the treatment of the subject. This was due to the fact that he instantly visualized the complete course of the action. He himself stated that in spirit he always sat in the auditorium while planning a play. And Scribe was a master not only of the art of arrangement, but of the no less difficult art of preparation. The public (as Legouvé keenly and aptly observes) is a very bizarre, exacting and inconsistent creature. In the theatre it would be prepared for anything and at the same time be surprised by everything. When a bolt falls from the blue, it is disquieted; when an

event is too distinctly forecast, it is bored.
So we must both take it into our confidence
and—fool it; that is, at some point in the drama
we must negligently introduce a brief and
wholly unexpected bit of information that
the auditor hears without paying attention
to it—a passing hint which, at the moment of
the grand climacteric effect, so charms him
that he inwardly exclaims: "Well, I was
forewarned against that—what an ass I was,
not to keep it in mind!" That is what the
public likes best of all. In this art Scribe
was a master, and in "Le Part du Diable" we
shall see just how he practised it.

Cleverness and skill, however, do not suffice
for the planning of a good plot; imagination is
also required, for within the plot are embraced the invention of the various turning-
points, or crises, the disposition of the dénouements, the intensification of suspense or
tension, the presentation of an idea in its
most effective form. No one (so reaffirms
Legouvé) ever possessed in a higher degree
than Scribe the talent for grasping a subject
in its most attractive aspect. It happened
that a friend once brought him a ponderous
five-act tragedy, which Scribe, while the friend
was reading it to him, transformed into a
charming one-act comedy. Scribe had instantly sensed the humorous side of the sub-

ject, and moulded it without more ado into the new, compressed form. Ah, were it only possible always to turn tiresome five-act tragedies into amusing one-act playlets!

Finally (observes Legouvé), the main point of a good plot is the dénouement. The art of dénouement in comedy is, in a certain sense, a modern art. True, Lope de Vega had already advanced it theoretically, though he had not applied it so skillfully in practice: "The subject must have only one plot. The story must not be interrupted by episodes or by other matters that stand in no connection with the principal action. One should not be able to subtract a single member from it, without thereby deranging the continuity of the whole. Begin weaving your plot from the start and continue to the close; the dénouement should not arrive until the last scene." In this matter the public has grown far more critical, and the authors have gained much experience, since (say) the time of Molière, who was still rather careless in this regard. Nowadays (proceeds Legouvé) one of the foremost dramatic rules is the requirement, that the dénouement should be the logical and necessary resultant of the characters or the events. For this reason the last scene of a piece is often written first; as long as the close is not invented, the play is unfinished, and as soon as the author knows what the end is to be, he must never lose sight of it and must make everything dependent on it. It was Scribe who best comprehended the importance of the dénouement, and who most implicitly followed its strictest laws. This, above all, distinguishes him from his predecessors.

Scribe's superiority lies in the invention of the subjects and their skillful disposition. He was less prominent (as Legouvé himself admits) as a stylist and an exponent of character. Like Beaumarchais, he apparently concentrated on the course of the action, being frequently indifferent to the wording. His characters are lacking in depth, and his personages are not drawn so true to life as Shakespeare's—they are mostly stage-humans. As a stylist and depicter of character Scribe must also rank below Molière, who often is his inferior in technic. Molière and Shakespeare wrote for all eternity, Scribe for the success of the hour. His style, often condensed and inelegant, he called the "style économique." For him the main thing was, that the short phrase "told" on the stage: theoretical objections were, in fact, nothing to him. And on that account he was an admirable librettist.

While Scribe was neglectful of style and characters, he laid principal stress on the last

point—the stage-management. Legouvé says
that a manuscript of Scribe's embodies nothing
but the spoken portion of the work; the rest is
played, gestures supplement the words, the
pauses are a part of the dialogue, and the
punctuation gives the final touch to the
phrasing. In Legouvé's opinion, there is a
sharp distinction between Scribe's punctuation
and Molière's; in particular, it was Scribe
who fathered the insertion of those "little
dots" (. . .) denoting the hesitant pause after
a half-finished sentence, and in this system of
little dots there lies an entire dramatic method,
so that Scribe was right in declaring the stage-
management to be a second creation forming, as
it were, a new play superimposed on the given
play. One ought (says Legouvé) to have
seen Scribe at rehearsal, where, like a general
on the battlefield, he took full command,
now improvising happily, now adding something new or cancelling something else.—In
France, a piece done in collaboration is really
finished only in the rehearsals, and usually
not printed until after the performance. No
wonder that the French dramatists are technically superior to those of all other national-
ities. In the case of musical works, too, one
might proceed similarly; we know how Berlioz
used to try all manner of experiments during
rehearsals, till the right thing was found; and

anyone who has assisted at Gustav Mahler's private rehearsals knows how this sensitive conductor was continually contriving new effects in his own works. The old saying that practice makes perfect is nowhere more applicable than in theatrical matters.

The story of "Le Part du Diable"[1] is a bit of original invention, though founded on an historical incident. Carlo Broschi (called Farinelli), the hero of the opera (born in Naples, June 24, 1705, died in Bologna, July 15, 1782), was possibly the greatest singer of the eighteenth century—a castrato, about whose marvellous singing wondrous tales are told. It is likewise an historical fact that Broschi cured King Philip V of Spain of his deep melancholy by singing to him, at the instance of Queen Elizabeth, a princess of Ferrara. It may be added that the king's melancholy was induced by the death of a son—here Scribe deviates. He lays the scene of the action (probably on account of the plot) in the time of this king's predecessor, Ferdinand VI, and of his queen, Maria Theresia of Portugal. How Scribe originally approached this subject can best be learned from his novel, "Carlo Broschi" (Œuvres complètes, Vol. IV, p. 55; Paris, 1859), in which that famous singer is also the central figure, although the story of the opera

[1] "The Devil's Portion."

and that of the novel coincide only in a very short passage near the end.

In his novel, Scribe lets the king's barber tell the following anecdote: "At the beginning of his reign the king was tormented by an illness that nothing could cure. Señor Xuniga, the court physician, had lavished all his art upon it, only to discover that this disease had a strong affinity to one which (as he said) was invented by the English, and which he called 'the spleen.' The king had already twice attempted his own life without assignable reason, and, despite the queen's distraction and the admonitions of Father Anastasius, his father-confessor, it was to be feared that our exalted sovereign would finally succeed in a design which would entail his perdition in this world and the next. For a month he had shut himself up in his apartment, refusing to see anyone excepting the queen, and in spite of her entreaties and expostulations he obstinately rejected all proffered services, even such as were most beneficial for his health and comfort; thus he stubbornly refused to change his underclothing or to allow himself to be shaved! . . . We were all in despair, the queen likewise. She devotedly loved her spouse, yet, seeing his reason and his very life threatened by the gloom of brooding melancholy, she knew no remedy that might save him therefrom, until she suddenly thought of Farinelli, whose voice, so it was said, worked miracles. She begged him to come to Madrid; he was conveyed into a room next the king's. At the first tones of that heavenly voice, the king trembled! 'That is an angel-voice!' he cried. And he listened intently; then, profoundly affected, he fell on his knees and wept, something that had never happened during his illness. 'Once more!' he exclaimed, 'once more! I must hear those tones again that have refreshed me and recalled me to life!' Farinelli sang again, and the king, now completely restored, threw himself into the queen's arms; thereupon bursting into the adjoining room, he embraced Farinelli with the exclamation: 'My angel! my deliverer! whoever thou art, ask of me what thou wilt, I'll give it thee—only demand, I will grant it!' And Farinelli responded: 'I beg that Your Majesty will change your underclothing and let yourself be shaved!' "

This little anecdote, a commixture of the story of Saul and David and the episode between Alexander the Great and Diogenes, was the embryo out of which grew Auber's exciting libretto. Now let us investigate how the ingenious Scribe went about his task. In the first place there was, ready to hand, a

tremendously effective situation to be wrought
up into a musical and dramatic climax;—the
melancholy king is restored to life by the
divinely beautiful strains of a youthful singer,
and would reward the singer in princely
fashion. Beside the king, his loving queen,
whose sole desire is the deliverance of her
spouse. Thus we already have three principals
in the action—King, Queen, Singer. A fourth
person, the king's father-confessor, is also
named; of him Scribe made a representative
of gloomy Spanish fanaticism, an inquisitor
and—intriguer. By this means Scribe obtained a splendid conductor of the "counter-
intrigue," and a special effect at the culmin-
ation of the action (close of the second act).
The plotting of the inquisitor is, to begin with,
of a political nature, directed against the
queen as a foreigner. Later (in accordance
with the counter-intriguer's churchly office)
he continues his plotting under the mantle of
religion, and this from the moment, as we
shall see, when the inquisitor recognizes Carlo
as his chief opponent. Carlo, as the deliverer of the king and, at the same time, of
the queen, is the best foil for the inquisitor.
Thus we have, as affecting the king, the
conflict of two influences; on the one side
fights the inquisitor, on the other the queen
with Carlo's assistance. But the inquisitor

must also have a helper, this being one Gil
Vargas, whose fearsomeness as the inquisitor's
accomplice is in the end fully outweighed by
the comicality of his behavior, the atmosphere
of comedy being thus preserved. Now arises
the question, By what means did the inquisitor
seek to dominate the king and to estrange
him from the queen? Answer: With Vargas's
connivance he attempted to press upon him
as mistress an innocent young girl, with whom
the king fell in love, and whom the inquisitor
forcibly conducted to the king through the
instrumentality of Vargas. But this young
girl—in love with another man, of course—
quickly escaped from the toils and fled. Now
Scribe also discovers a convincing reason for the
king's melancholy; the king believes the maiden
to be dead, hence the disorder of his mind.
Is not this clever? But better is to come!
The young maiden, who (of course) has no
idea that the *king* was pursuing her, and who
had seen no one save Vargas, has (as noted
above) a secret lover whose name and rank
she does not know (observe how the action
turns on these secrets, and how ingeniously
Scribe makes it all quite plausible); he had
introduced himself, in the millinery establish-
ment where the girl is engaged, simply as a
student of theology. This lover is, in reality,
a Spanish grandee, Rafael de Estuniga, sole

heir to an immense fortune, which may be his
after the demise of an uncle now on his death-
bed.   So we have a love-affair, into the bargain.
Now notice how astutely Scribe interweaves
all these nicely disposed threads.   Rafael's
teacher is none other than the theologian
Vargas, the inquisitor's helper; this is a connecting-link between the "intrigue" and the
"counter-intrigue"; and the young girl, pur-
sued by the king and beloved by Rafael, is
nobody but—the sister of Carlo Broschi!
Thereby a wholly new connecting-link is introduced into the plot; Carlo moves the
melancholy monarch not merely by any chance
song, but by one very special song known only
to himself and his sister.   And this song it was
that the king had once heard sung by Casilda,
Carlo's sister.   This accounts for the brooding
king's emotion.   The song, whose music and
words are so devised as to be available in the
most momentous situations of the subsequent
action, will naturally play a leading part in
all three acts.   Herewith the plot is already
quite clearly indicated, and the principal
conflicts and developments established.   But
now Scribe had another happy thought, which
adds just the needful spice to the refection.
It is evident that the fate of Rafael and Casilda
lies in the hands of Carlo, and that he must
take a continuously active part in the course

of events. How does Scribe bring this about? With a wholly admirable trick of prestidigitation. While Carlo is really the nephew of that enormously rich uncle, it is said uncle's intention, in the very shadow of death, to disinherit his nephew because, instead of studying theology, he spends his money for fine raiment and feminine adornments, besides running into debt. For Rafael is a full-blooded nobleman of a martial line, who therefore would rather have joined the army; but his attempt to obtain an ensigncy miscarries. So he finds himself in a tight place, with only one way of escape—to sell his soul to the Devil. In guise of the Devil, however, there appears—Carlo Broschi, who has learned by eavesdropping that Rafael is his sister's lover. Rafael strikes a bargain with the "Devil" on a fifty-fifty basis. Thus the way is cleared for the full swing of Scribe's humorous fancy. Rafael (who finally sees his dearest wishes fulfilled through happy accidents and Carlo's omnipotence at court) has to go halves with the "Devil" in everything; in money, in honors, and lastly even in—his wife. But he also bears with equanimity the less pleasing aspects of life, such as imprisonment and mortal danger, for the risk is not his alone, as he shares everything with his fiendish copartner. Scribe turns all the possible complications to the best account, and is inexhaustible in his invention of situations bringing Rafael (and Carlo with him) continually into new difficulties, out of which, however, they always unexpectedly find their way when the danger is at its height. Thus Scribe rivets our attention till the last moment; further on we shall have an opportunity to admire the masterly fashion in which he gradually looses the knot. Here only the lines were to be shown, along which the action progresses, and it was my purpose to suggest the mental processes through which Scribe probably developed his complicated comedy out of a very simple anecdote. We have, in fact, thus come at all the characters with the sole exception of the Count of Medrano, a mere "walking gentleman's" part.

Having indicated how the plot took shape in Scribe's mind, let us proceed to construct the entire scenario after his method, so as to penetrate deeper into the finer details of his work.

Act I

First of all, the setting of the scenery is a masterpiece of Scribe's constructive talent: "Wooded region in the environs of Madrid. To the right, a convent; to the left, a tavern; in the centre of the stage a great oak, whose branches hang down to the ground, concealing a stone seat placed beneath them."

This has a matter-of-course air, but is really the outcome of much subtle meditation: How shall I bring my characters together in one place without letting them inopportunely fall foul of one another? Nothing simpler than that, says Scribe; to begin with, here we have the main property, the Devil's Oak (for a regular Devil lets himself be invoked only in a proper, diabolically infected, spot); and this tree with its concealed seat is equally well adapted as a screen for Carlo's eavesdropping. On the right is a convent—ostensibly, merely to vex the Devil, as is casually suggested, but in reality the absconded Casilda dwells in this convent, so she is conveniently at hand, like her brother Carlo, who lavishes his gifts of song in payment of his sister's board and lodging. Now only the king and queen have to be provided for. Well, to-day the court goes a-hunting in the forest, for the diversion of the melancholy monarch; so they both soon appear, accompanied by the inevitable inquisitor, and the tavern on the left does not merely form a very pretty decoration, but is, like every stage tavern, eminently practical as a place into which to dismiss any persons for whom one has no immediate use on the stage. It possesses the peculiar advantage that anybody, without regard to rank, can be hustled into such a forest inn—whether king or beggar, it's all the same. So Scribe says to himself, Why shouldn't there be a tavern just here, when the world is full of taverns?—and again hits the nail on the head. And now, assisted so far as possible by Legouvé's revelations concerning Scribe's technic, let us examine how cleverly the French wizard planned his play.

Scene 1

Rafael, Vargas

We hear that the wealthy uncle is dissatisfied with Rafael and Vargas because the former has learned nothing and the latter has taught nothing. Rafael confesses that he has fallen in love with a young modiste whom he saw, opposite his house, in the shop of Señora Uracca, the leading milliner of Madrid, and that he has also run into debt on her account. He is resolved to renounce theology and, in order to win his sweetheart, to make his way with the sword—if need be, in alliance with the Devil. This very day, St. John's day, is the right time, and at ten o'clock in the evening (this somewhat early hour is chosen to motivate the entrance of the king shortly before) the Devil may be invoked beside

this tree—at least, so it is written in an old
book. Vargas has his doubts, and advises him
to apply to the Grand Inquisitor, who is coming hither to-night in attendance on the king.
For a hunt by torchlight has been arranged for
the king's diversion. During this dialogue
Scribe ingeniously puts a whole series of
significant hints into Vargas's mouth, which
do not materialize until Scene 5 (in Act II).
Here we learn for the present only the bare
essentials: Vargas knows exactly why the
king is melancholy, and under the seal of
secrecy informs his pupil as follows: "There
was a young maiden, for whose death he believes himself to blame, and whose shade
persistently pursues him. The Grand Inquisitor, Fray Antonio, confidant and favorite of
the wretched monarch, had a hand in this
affair. . . . He is indebted to me for important services rendered in very delicate and
dangerous matters, and has promised to reward
me for them. As soon as he shall succeed
in separating the queen from her spouse and
sending her back to Portugal, my fortune is
made. For this reason I hope that he will
not fail to exert his mighty influence in hehalf
of my pupil."—In order to formulate this
petition to the Grand Inquisitor, they both go
off into the tavern. Thus (according to
Legouvé) Scribe at once takes us into his con-

fidence and mystifies us; we hear about important matters without having an inkling of their importance, for so far the king, queen, inquisitor and young girl mean nothing to us. We are interested, at most, in the love-affair and career of Rafael. That his beloved modiste is identical with the young maiden for whom the king mourns, never enters our heads.

Scene 2

Carlo *alone*

He has been an involuntary listener to the dialogue hard by the tree beneath which he had composed himself to sleep. Rafael's lot excites his pity, for it seems to resemble his own, Carlo likewise being without friends, fortune, and hope. Yet he bids defiance to fate, knowing that a beloved sister needs his care; for her he will contend, trusting that ill fortune may be averted.

Scene 3

Carlo, Casilda

Casilda comes out of the convent to greet Carlo. He asks her to tell him why she left Madrid so hurriedly and fled hitherward; he had not been able to understand her letter (naturally, he says this only that the audience may have an opportunity to be fully informed). It is a clever trick (however improbable) to let Carlo apparently forget the name of the house in Madrid where he had obtained lodgings for his sister; and it is only when Casilda mentions the name of the milliner Uracca that he glimpses (as do we ourselves) a connection between the conversation he has just overheard and the present one. So now we know that Rafael loves Casilda, and that Casilda is Carlo's sister. Rafael, however, is ignorant of Casilda's name and rank, precisely as she herself is unaware that her lover is a young theologian. Then we hear about another incident (without, of course, knowing in the least that it supplements the story of abduction previously told by Vargas); Casilda tells her brother how, seated by the window, she was wont to sing songs, in particular "that lullaby of our dear departed mother's" (highly important!). One day she was applauded by two disguised cavaliers, who since than had . passed by every evening; and one morning came an elderly man of most respectable appearance (no one guesses that this was Vargas!), who induced her, urged thereto by her employer, to drive with him in an equipage to a high-born lady who, on account of an indisposition, desired to have her measure taken in her palace. But his real purpose was the abduction of Casilda to put her in the hands of a "young cavalier of noble mien" (nobody dreams that the king is meant!). Casilda, however, succeeded in escaping and found her way to this tavern, whence she wrote her brother, who procured her reception into the convent under condition that Carlo should sing in the church for a year without remuneration. Yet her heart still yearns for the young theologian, fearing never to see him more. Carlo soothes her, but at the same time hints that her lover's high rank presents an apparently insuperable obstacle to their union. She must hope for better days, for their mother's spirit is watching over them. Exit Casilda into convent.

Scene 4

Carlo *alone*

Carlo remains behind. Having not yet broken his fast, he would like to enter the tavern, but that is too dear for him. What little money he possesses he would rather give his sister. Finding that he still has a morsel of bread, he designs to eat it *al fresco* and alone. Alone? No, he is not alone; his mother's spirit hovers ever above him. (Observe how Scribe accounts for Carlo's remaining, and also how he motivates Carlo's singing of that particular lullaby during the following scene.)

Scene 5

King, Queen, Carlo (*concealed on the stone seat*)

After this exposition of the situation in which Rafael and Casilda find themselves, Scribe brings on the king änd queen, to intertwine their fortunes with Carlo's. The vision-haunted king enters, leaning on the queen's arm, and again sees the apparition (regarding which he leaves the queen in ignorance, though we know what it is from Vargas's story). Now he hears the voice of Carlo, who, his thoughts fixed on his mother, sings a phrase from the lullaby. The King is startled, for he fancies that the young maiden whom he thinks dead is repeating the song. He asks who it is that sings, and bids the youthful singer approach, the latter not dreaming who it is that requests him to sing the entire song. Carlo explains that the song is his mother's lullaby, and sings the two strophes of which it is composed. Now observe with care how Scribe constructed this song. The first strophe is nothing more nor less than a real lullaby:

Ferme ta paupière,	Close thine eyelids,
Dors, mon pauvre enfant,	Sleep, my poor child,
Ne vois pas ta mère	Look not on thy mother,
Qui prie en pleurant.	Who prays all in tears.

Dame noble et fière,	Lady noble and proud,
Belle Señora,	Lovely Señora,
Calmez ma misère	Relieve my misery,
Et Dieu vous le rendra.	And God will reward you.
‖: Donnez, donnez sur cette terre,	Give, give here on earth,
Dieu dans le ciel vous donnera.: ‖	God in heaven will give reward.

The most important part of this song is the refrain: "Give here on earth, God in heaven will give reward," a petition which now, as sung for the first time, is directed at the Madonna, but—and this is the dramatically significant point—in the further course of the action is directed at the king himself.

In the second act Carlo, when his life is threatened, sings before the king's cabinet the same melody to the words:

Ô roi de la terre,	O king of the earth,
Ô noble Seigneur,	O noble lord,
Entends la prière	Hear the prayer
De ton serviteur;	Of thy servant;
Si trop téméraire	If all too boldly
Ma voix s'élèvera,	My voice be raised,
En toi seul j'espère,	In thee alone I hope,
Car ta clémence est là.	For clemency is thine.
‖: A qui pardonne sur la terre,	To him who pardons here on earth,
Dieu dans le ciel pardonnera.: ‖	God in heaven shall pardon give.

It is evident that the words of this song are a mere adaptation of the second strophe of the song heard in Act I, here accommodated to the dramatic situation.

In Act II the king is not only reminded by the melody of his own grievous transgression against Casilda, but is at the same time adjured by the words to give aid, so that his helpful intervention is well motivated. This song is the impelling force at the most important turning-point in the drama, for which reason its translation requires very special care, so that the meaning of the drama itself may not be perverted.

The king thanks Carlo, and asks him to name a boon; Carlo answers (as in the anecdote given above) that he would beg the sovereign to have beard and hair put in seemly order, to don raiment more befitting and more in keeping with the beautiful lady beside him— a very shrewd stroke, which raises him still higher in the queen's favor.

Scene 6

The same; Inquisitor *and* Courtiers

The king salutes the gentlemen and avers that he has not felt so well in a long time. "That is a bad sign, an ill omen for us," remarks the inquisitor aside. The king, however, desires to rest yet a while in the tavern, so he invites his train to enter with him. The queen alone begs to be excused for a moment (in order to speak with Carlo, of course).

Scene 7

The Queen, Carlo

The queen questions Carlo as to his name and family relations, whereby we, too, learn something further about them. She proposes to take Carlo to Madrid, but he declines the offer because of his sister, whom "a high-born gentleman of Madrid had attempted to abduct and seduce." The queen says that Carlo ought to demand justice of the king, but Carlo replies that the king is crazy, though the queen's heart is in the right place. Thereupon she discovers herself to him. Carlo implores her pardon, and now the queen straightway undertakes to care for his sister, and orders him to follow her as soon as he has informed the Abbess of her plan. In all this Carlo again recognizes his mother's protecting love. Exit into convent; the queen remains.

Scene 8

The Queen, Rafael, Vargas

Just here we have another little conjurer's trick of Scribe's, which the audience, however, never notices;—in the first scene Vargas had advised Rafael to write a petition to the Grand Inquisitor, who (it is taken for granted) is the power behind the throne. Now, how does Rafael come to request a recommendation to the queen from the inquisitor, her enemy, and why, at the beginning of this scene, does Vargas send Rafael to the queen? Scribe's only reason could have been to bring directly before our eyes the refusal of the appointment to the ensigncy by the personage next in power to the king, and thus to make his subsequent fabulous rise the more remarkable. Rafael approaches the queen, and petitions as a nobleman for an ensigncy in the Netherlands. The queen is on the point of granting it, when Rafael produces the recommendation of the inquisitor. The queen instantly closes the audience coldly and ironically: "One whom my enemies recommend, no longer needs my protection." She follows the king into the tavern, whither Vargas had preceded her.

Scene 10

Rafael; Huntsmen *passing over*

While the huntsmen sing their jovial ditty, Rafael is a prey to despair. Even the powerful inquisitor had availed him nothing—earth and heaven have conspired together against him.

Scene 11

Rafael *alone*

Rafael's resolve is fixed—hell must grant
him what heaven refuses. Ten o'clock strikes.
Time and place are favorable, and he begins
his incantation. But Asmodeus, however
courteously or rudely besought, fails to appear;
even the Devil, it seems, will have nothing
to do with him.

Scene 12

Rafael, Carlo

Carlo comes unnoticed out of the convent
and hears Rafael's incantation; but not until
Rafael vows to the Devil that he will kill
himself, does Carlo venture to impersonate
Satan—truly, a strange imitation of Satan,
who secretly begs the good Lord's forgiveness
for the deception. Indeed, when he comes as
a genuine Devil to demand Rafael's soul, he
trembles more than Rafael does at his sin.
But Rafael notices nothing, although he
hesitates to give his soul in pawn. Instead,
he offers the Devil to go halves with him,
which the latter declares to be bad business,
but finally accepts. "The half of everything,
whatever it be!" is the agreement. First of
all Rafael wants the ensigncy. The Devil

objects, that this cannot be divided; still, he will get it for him, provided he demeans himself decorously and discreetly. It strikes Rafael as decidedly odd that the Devil should preach morality to him, but now the royal chase is nearing, and they must break off the conversation. Carlo wraps himself in his clock and disappears among the royal train. The torches of the huntsmen, awaiting the king here, light up the hitherto dark stage. Curtain.

Evidently, this act is merely an exposition; all the more eager is our expectation of the following events. "Le Part du Diable" is less an "opera" than a comedy with music, as the earlier *opéra comique* (comedy-opera) was so frequently a *comédie mêlée d'ariettes* (comedy interspersed with ariettas), the music being interpolated, as it were, in the dialogue. Thus, in this particular act, arias and romances (songs) have the upper hand; Rafael and Carlo have their arias, Casilda and Carlo their romances; besides these there are only two duets (between Casilda and Carlo, Carlo and Rafael) and the short Hunting-chorus; lengthy ensembles are wanting.

ACT II

Hall in the Royal Palace at Madrid
Three months later

Scene I

King, Queen, Carlo (*in rich page-costume*),
Chorus

The king sleeps; the fever that once tormented him is wholly allayed since Carlo's voice revived him. However, happy as this has made the queen, a new sorrow oppresses her, which she confides to Carlo;—her secret enemy, the Grand Inquisitor, is seeking to reëstablish his influence over the king; to-day he will preach a great sermon, and the king has promised to attend. Ten o'clock strikes, the king awakes, and would go to hear the sermon, the inquisitor having reminded him of it; but Carlo, in league with the queen, sings to the mandolin a joyous Neapolitan song, whose wit is rightly communicable only in the original French. The song is about a melancholy countess to whom is sent a Neapolitan physician. "Ah, je vous supplie, prenez ce médecin napolitain d'un savoir certain" (Ah, I implore you, receive this Neapolitan physician, whose skill is assured.") The "melancholy countess" is naturally an allusion to the king himself, and the "Neapolitan physician" none other than Carlo. In vain does the inquisitor urge the king to attend the sermon; Carlo continually interrupts with a continuation of the joyous ditty, which charms the king. Meantime the sermon comes to an end, but this troubles the king not at all; that can be repeated, he observes, but now Carlo shall go on with his song. The song so strengthens his heart that he proposes to-day to preside over the State Council again for the first time, to the joy of the queen, to the rage of the inquisitor. Exeunt omnes, except the queen and Carlo.

Scene 2

Carlo, the Queen

The queen expresses her gratitude to Carlo for the miracle he has wrought with the king. The latter, however, is not fully restored; sometimes (the queen says) some secret oppresses him, and he is seized by frenzied convulsions. No songs help him then, only the one that Carlo once sang in the forest never fails of effect (we know why this is so, but the queen and Carlo have no idea). But Carlo, too, is often sad, and the queen guesses the reason—he cannot bear to be separated from his beloved sister. So the queen will send for the sister immediately, but she must bear a title at court. Therefore, the queen creates her "Signora Theresa di Belmonte," and makes Carlo Court Conductor. The Master of Ceremonies, Count Medrano, is to fetch Casilda and escort her hither by the secret stairway; Carlo is to await her here, and then bring her to the queen. Again take note how Scribe prepares matters. Carlo has one objection—*one* person at court knows Casilda, and this person is Rafael. Now we also learn of Rafael's further fortunes; through Carlo's intercession he has after all obtained, to his vast astonishment, his ensigncy from the queen herself; has fought bravely, and for that reason has been entrusted by his general with a message to the queen, which he is to deliver this same morning. The queen already has in mind a distinction to be conferred on him (what it is, she does not divulge), and Carlo confides to her that Rafael loves his sister deeply and truly, and that he (Carlo) loves Rafael like a brother. But, in Carlo's opinion, the lovers can probably never be united. Now consider how everything is prepared. We know that Rafael is coming to the queen and will receive a distinction; we also know that Casilda is to be introduced as maid-of-honor to the queen; and we have been told how the king still suffers at times from the delirious fancy that the young maiden has lost her life. Thus we are prepared for all the following events—and nevertheless, the sensational *manner* in which Scribe introduces them positively astounds us, as we have pretty much lost sight of "the Devil's portion," although Carlo calls our attention to it with a casual remark, "He probably thinks his commission came from hell."

Scene 3

The same; Rafael

Enter Rafael in ensign's uniform. The queen pretends to be provoked that the general sent a mere ensign; the blunder must be remedied: "Arise, *Captain* Rafael!" Rafael is astonished, but in a moment he catches sight of Carlo; "Asmodeus" is "on the job," so nothing further surprises him, not even the purse of gold pieces given him by the queen for his equipment.

Scene 4

Rafael, Carlo

Rafael's first thought is to employ the money in travelling throughout Spain in search of his beloved modiste. But Carlo upsets the plan; the Devil's portion must be paid—to Rafael the honor, to Asmodeus the cash. Rafael finds it a rather hard bargain, but a nobleman must keep his word, especially in view of the fact that the Devil has already promoted him to a captaincy. Exit Carlo.

Scene 5

Rafael, Vargas

In the Doorkeeper of the palace Rafael recognizes his old teacher Vargas (another clever trick of Scribe's); this modest post was the only one that the inquisitor could procure for his protégé, and Vargas is lost in wonder that Rafael should enjoy such high protection, for Vargas, being a spy for the inquisitor, must keep his eye on everything. Now, as Vargas tells his woes to Rafael, we learn still more about past events. Vargas narrates: "First I took service with your uncle; then I gave myself body and soul to the Grand Inquisitor. He, who had vainly sought a means to estrange the king from the queen, suddenly discovered that the king had fallen in love with a young maiden whom he had seen at a window opening on his park, and heard singing (take note— *singing!*). He ordered me to abduct her and carry her off to Aranjuez. I carried out this delicate and honorable mission most successfully; but a quarter of an hour after her arrival in the castle, the young maiden had fled, and was nowhere to be found. Now, what was to be done? The king was told that she was dead, and it was this story that caused his incurable melancholy."—Now, all at once, we begin to see clear; the tale told by

Casilda in Act I, which, so far as we could then see, had no connection with the dark hints thrown out by Vargas, suddenly takes on an entirely new meaning;—Casilda is the young maiden for whom the king mourns. Here it dawns upon us, what a triple rôle Casilda has to play as Rafael's sweetheart, Carlo's sister, and the king's phantom. It is just this interweaving of three activities interpreted by one and the same personage that Scribe carries through with technical mastership. From this important conversation of Vargas with Rafael we learn still more; the inquisitor's influence is ebbing, and in case his covert intrigues should be brought to light, he intends throwing all the blame on Vargas, whose mind is consequently ill at ease (note this excellent motivation of Vargas's desertion to the opposing party in Act III). The once almighty inquisitor has been ousted by an unknown young man who has ingress to the king at any time, unannounced. Rafael does not find this strange; he lets Vargas know that this young man is Asmodeus, the Prince of Darkness. Vargas hesitates to believe this, but Rafael shows him his captain's commission, just obtained by Asmodeus' intervention. Vargas now appears to be convinced, but counsels Rafael to beware of the Inquisition.

Scene 6

The same; Officers of the Guard

Enter Officers, to play at dice. Vargas is invited by Rafael to play with the latter's money, but loses a large sum—of course, for he does not stand under Asmodeus' protection. Then Rafael plays himself, and—immediately wins.

Scene 7

The same; Carlo

Rafael is about to pocket his winnings, when Carlo claps him on the shoulder and demands the Devil's portion. Vargas has followed all this with dubious mien, and makes up his mind to get at the bottom of the matter (preparation for what is to follow).

Scene 8

The same; *without* Officers

Carlo looks upon the money he takes from Rafael as a sort of trust account which he is carrying for Rafael; whereas Vargas naturally believes Carlo to be an adventurer seeking wealth at Rafael's expense. Rafael, however, explains to Vargas that nothing is impossible to his protector. Whereupon Vargas asks

Rafael to let his conjurer display his magic art then and there, and Carlo thinks to himself, Now the Devil's in for it! when Rafael demands nothing less of Asmodeus than to let him again behold that unknown beauty, whom he loves. Hardly have the words left his mouth, and— the secret door flies open and Casilda, with the Master of Ceremonies, stands before Rafael.

Scene 9
The same; Casilda, Count Medrano

Scribe could not have timed Casilda's entrance more delectably. Consider, that for Rafael and Vargas her sudden appearance has the effect of magic; for Carlo, too, her entrance is quite unexpected; but the audience has really been taken into Scribe's confidence (we have been told that Casilda is to be conducted to the queen)—and fooled. And for Vargas, as well, the situation is very peculiar; he is quite as surprised as Rafael (as the latter remarks), "and not without reason," as Vargas dryly observes, for Casilda is that same young girl whom he had spirited away. Rafael wishes to embrace Casilda, but the Master of Ceremonies interposes; and—as the Devil has no use for half of a Master of Ceremonies—Carlo refuses to expel him at Rafael's request. So Rafael, by reiterated refusal to obey the

Count's orders, has one day after another added to his guard-house sentence, with comical effect, until the Count, acting by virtue of his disciplinary powers as governor of the palace, gives him eight days (though Rafael fancies that the Devil's portion reduces the sentence by half). Exit Rafael on his way to the guard-house, while Vargas resolves to win over this mysterious coadjutor for the Inquisition: "I do not know, indeed, whether he is a sorcerer or not, but at all events it can do no harm to exorcize him." Medrano entrusts the sister to Carlo's care, and exit to queen.

Scene 10

Carlo, Casilda

A scene brief in time, but highly significant. Carlo tells Casilda that by the queen's command they are not to conduct themselves here as brother and sister. Casilda has not only joyfully recognized Rafael, but has instantly detected in Vargas the man "of perfidious mien and jesuitical gaze" who was her abductor. Carlo (who naturally hasn't the faintest notion that the king has a hand in the game) advises her to throw herself at the feet of the entering monarch and to implore justice against her betrayer.

Scene 11

The same; the King

Most dramatic situation; in Casilda the king recognizes the lost maiden, Casilda in him the cavalier into whose hands she had been betrayed. This she hastily communicates to her brother; the king on his part does not conceal from Carlo that Casilda is the apparition which robs him of all repose. Only with difficulty is Carlo able to convince the king that the young maiden is alive, and no phantom.

The king strictly enjoins Carlo to observe secrecy concerning his wrongdoing, for which Heaven now punishes him with remorse.

Scene 12

The same; the Queen

The queen's entrance renders the situation still more unpleasant for the king. Carlo tells her in a hurried whisper that he has now discovered the cause of the king's enigmatic sufferings, and the queen desires to know it; but Carlo repents the hastily uttered words. The queen signifies that she awaits Carlo with his explanation; but the king, about to attend a State Council, also wishes speech with Carlo afterwards. The queen takes Casilda with her, the king goes off to the Council, Carlo remains behind by himself.

Scene 13

Carlo *alone*

A desperate situation, to be the confidant of both the king and queen, and at the same time brother of her whom the king loves! Neither is Rafael, as the king's rival, in an enviable position. It's lucky, remarks Carlo, that he is locked up for eight days, otherwise his rashness might spoil everything.

Scene 14

Carlo, Rafael

And at this very moment—enter Rafael (genuine comedy, this, he being the last person one would expect to see). So *you* can play the sorcerer! cries Carlo, dumfounded. As no arrangement had been made as to which of them should first serve his four days, Asmodeus or himself, Rafael had boldly risked a leap out of the window—the more boldly because "the Devil's portion" would let him off with only half the leap. He, of course, is seeking Casilda. Carlo intimates that he is acquainted with the earlier phases of his love-affair (which Rafael finds quite natural for the Devil), and advises him—self-evidently on the king's ac-count—to avoid his sweetheart, else ill fortune will dog his footsteps. Rafael makes light of this, so Carlo must have recourse to a last desperate expedient—that Casilda is of his own race, a child of the devil, and he must avoid her would he not devote his soul to eternal perdition.

Scene 15

The same; the Queen, Casilda

The queen returns with Casilda—of whom Rafael learns she is called Donna Theresa—it being her (the queen's) intention to proceed that same morning to Aranjuez. (Scribe thus skillfully removes the queen, so that she may not be able to aid the imperilled Carlo at the act-close.) Carlo has to accompany the queen to her carriage despite his reluctance (he does not wish to leave Rafael and Casilda alone together). Thus the scene is cleared for the lovers. Rafael learns from the queen's own mouth that Casilda is a new maid-of-honor, which strikes him as not strictly in keeping with her calling as a she-devil.

Scene 16

Rafael, Casilda

Rafael, comically wavering 'twixt love and his dread of hell, lets himself be led so far astray, in spite of Carlo's warning, as to sink down at Casilda's feet.

Scene 17

The same; the King, the Inquisitor

The king is enraged at finding the young officer at the feet of his inamorita, and at once has him arrested. (Very comical, that Rafael conceives this mishap merely as the result of his disobedience to Asmodeus.) But worse is in store; the inquisitor informs the king that it was Rafael who had been denounced as in league with the Devil, and the king directs the inquisitor to let the stringent law take its course. No one, under pain of death, is to enter his apartment. Exit king.

Scene 18

Rafael, the Inquisitor, Vargas, Halbardiers

Here Vargas's attitude is not quite clear; he has denounced Carlo for sorcery and must have been aware that Rafael was equally guilty. His excuse, that he thought Rafael was locked up (and therefore secure—why?), so that it was only Rafael's own foolishness in escaping from arrest that is to blame for bringing him to the stake, is not convincing. Here we have another of Scribe's clever tricks, wherewith the audience is duped. There is true comedy in the contrast between the direful prospect of being burned alive, and Rafael's demeanor, which remains easy and cheerful, for he feels that Asmodeus will again rescue him.

Scene 19

The same; Carlo

But now Carlo, too, is brought in under arrest. The danger is menacing—the queen in Aranjuez, the king, under guard of his halbardiers, inaccessible to all under pain of death, Carlo thus wholly in the power of his worst enemy, the inquisitor. Only one hope remains—to move the king by means of the well-known song. His last request, a prayer, cannot be refused by the inquisitor, and so Carlo sings the song, directed rather at the king than to God, as close as he can get to the king's cabinet. Hardly is the song at an end, when Carlo is seized to be carried off to his death; now the door of the cabinet opens, and the king steps out.

Scene 20

The same; the King

The situation takes a sudden turn, but only for Carlo, who is immediately set free by the king, for the order given the inquisitor does not apply to him. However, Carlo must also save Rafael. In an aside to the king he asks what crime Rafael has committed. The worst of all, answers the king; here, in the palace, he insulted the king by throwing himself at the feet of that young maiden. But Carlo is not slow in finding a pretext: Rafael, he replies to the king, had a right to do so, being —her husband. The king is thunderstruck; although the union is hateful to him, it is a legal one, and beyond his power to annul. Carlo gives the king the whispered advice, to send Rafael instantly out of the palace, that the king may regain his composure. But for the latter the thought is intolerable, that he might never see Casilda again, for Rafael would assuredly take his wife along. Now comes a genuine stroke *à la* Scribe—the king not only sets Rafael at liberty, but actually makes his excuses to him, and finally, to attach him to his own person, appoints him commander of his bodyguard! All of which is most astonishing to Vargas, while Rafael accepts even this new distinction as a matter of course. The inquisitor is routed, Carlo once more in favor, and Rafael triumphantly walks off with his old friend Vargas through the guardsmen and inquisitors.

In this brilliantly constructed act the cumulative effect of all the happy accidents, for which Rafael was apparently indebted to the art of "Asmodeus," is admirably felicitous.

The act reaches its musical climax in the grand finale (from Scene 18 onward), which is "through-composed," and one of the most valuable numbers of the score. · For the rest, this act does not offer the musician very many opportunities, but these are very favorable. The first scene, with Carlo's merry Neapolitan ditty, is delightful; less important, though very pretty, is the gaming scene; least prominent is the Quartet in Scene 11, whereas the duet between Rafael and Casilda (Scene 16) is really charming. But the contrast in the finale between the gruesome and the comical presents one of the most favorable opportunities which the poet can offer the musician.

Act III

Here again Scribe is inexhaustible in his invention of novel shifts. The scene is laid in the castle at Aranjuez, in a hall having a view over the royal gardens.

Scene 1

Carlo *alone*

Carlo is awaiting the queen, whom he had entreated to meet him here. He feels anxious for Casilda and himself as regards their future, for, even if the king is continually deceived by his courtiers, he (Carlo) cannot bear to think that he imposed upon his sovereign, even in his utmost need. He hopes the queen can advise him what further steps to take.

Scene 2

Carlo, the Queen

The queen fancies that she knows Carlo's secret, and this occasions her to tell another secret—certain persons are trying to persuade the king to put her away; there are rumors of a divorce and a new marriage with the daughter of the king of Sardinia. It is even said that the inquisitor, Fray Antonio, is a hireling of the Sardinian court, with which he carries on a clandestine correspondence through the medium of one of his agents, Gil Vargas. Of this plot Carlo offers to furnish the queen with the proofs she urgently requires. Notice here that the intelligence of the inquisitor's connection with the Sardinian court is news for us, but as we had already heard of the inquisitor's machinations against the queen, and of Vargas's collusion, these latest disclosures do not come as a complete surprise.

Carlo entreats that, first of all, Rafael and Casilda may be married; this will not be difficult, for a word from the queen would induce Rafael's wealthy old uncle to change his mind. Now a new obstacle arises—the old uncle (so the queen has heard) has just died without disinheriting Rafael, but Rafael has thereby fallen heir to so vast a fortune that he can scarcely be expected further to consider a marriage with Casilda. In any event (Carlo implores), let the queen tell the king, in case he should bring up the subject of their marriage, that she herself had been present at their wedding. Their conversation must be abruptly broken off, before the queen has time to find out the reason for this new request of Carlo's (very clever!).

Scene 3

Carlo, Rafael, Vargas

Carlo devoutly hopes that Rafael may not hear of his uncle's death until the wedding is an accomplished fact. But, behold! in comes the rascally Vargas, bringing Rafael the news, and adding that with the inherited 600,000 ducats he might aspire to the hand of a princess. Carlo, however, reminds him that "the Devil's portion" amounts to 300,000 ducats, reducing his inheritance by half! This fairly infuriates Vargas against the "crafty imposter," whom he resolves to put to the test at once. Rafael, as officer of the Guard, is called away by a drum-signal to form the lane for the reception of the queen. Vargas, to whom this reception is "of no consequence" (this seems hardly plausible in a Doorkeeper), takes advantage of the king's entrance (now going on in the rear) to sneak up behind Carlo, who is seated at a table, writing, and present a pistol at his head with the query, whether the mighty magician knows what is going to happen to him the very next moment. Carlo replies coolly that he cannot foretell his own fate, but can prophesy Vargas's as the abductor of a young maiden whom he intended to betray into the king's hands—he will be hanged this same evening by order of the queen, who is about to sign his death-warrant; still, he can save himself by giving up the letters from the Sardinian court to the inquisitor. Vargas does not hesitate long to hand over the letter which he happens to have by him, reasoning that (as he has seen in Rafael's case) "Asmodeus" is prompter than the inquisitor in coming to the aid of his protégés. Rafael, on his return, is astounded to find his teacher already in the power of the Prince of Darkness—who is, to be sure, rather expensive, but very punctual. Rafael makes one last request of "Asmodeus"—he wishes to take to wife that "she-devil," Casilda, immediately and without further ado.

Scene 4

The same; Count Medrano

Here Scribe introduces another typical effect. Although we are aware that Carlo (in the preceding act) designated Rafael to the king as Casilda's spouse, and although we know that only a few minutes ago he entreated the queen to tell the king that she had been present at their wedding, we are no less surprised than Rafael by the bomb-like irruption of a letter in the royal handwriting. The king writes: "You are married, this we know. It is, therefore, our will, that this very evening you should occupy the apartments set aside for you in our palace, with Donna Theresa, your spouse." So Rafael, as the king says so, has been married "without having noticed it."

Scene 5

The same; the King

Now the king enters on his progress and congratulates Rafael, approving the marriage. Rafael can find words only to inquire from whom the king had received the information. —From Carlo and the queen, who had herself been present at the wedding.

Scene 6

Rafael, Carlo, Vargas

Rafael is naturally more and more astonished; but it is really all the same to him when, where and how he was married—the main point is, he has been married, whereof there can be no doubt, as the queen herself was present. But now matters are at a critical pass for Carlo's sister, as Rafael would forthwith hasten to his bride. Again Carlo has a happy thought—only half of Casilda belongs to Rafael, for, according to their agreement, the Devil reserved half of everything. But this is a little too much for Rafael—the Devil is welcome to the whole of Vargas, to square accounts, but as for sharing his wife with "Asmodeus"—never!

Scene 7

The same; Casilda

At this moment Casilda enters (ingenious motivation of her coming, and of Carlo's departure: at the close of Scene 2 the queen told Carlo that in a while, after the reception of an ambassador, she would send Casilda to call Carlo). She says to Carlo that the queen awaits him. In an aside—in order that the audience may not get wind of the new trick—

Carlo arranges with her that, so long as she is together with Rafael, she should (to protect herself) conduct herself as if in presence of the Devil. To this Casilda reluctantly assents. Exeunt Carlo and Vargas on their way to the queen.

Scene 8

Rafael, Casilda

One of the most charming scenes in the opera; whenever Rafael would be tender, Casilda "registers" the Devil's participation in her, asserting that the Devil is showing her the same fond attention from the other side— whereat Rafael finally becomes enraged.

Scene 9

The same; the King

Enter king; Rafael, deluded by the phantom devil, falls at his feet before Casilda can interpose, and craves the boon of a real marriage-ceremony.

Scene 10

The same; the Queen, Inquisitor, Vargas

The king's ire is turned against the queen, who had assured him of her presence at the wedding.

Scene .11

The same; Carlo

All eyes are fixed upon Carlo. Height of the tension, just before the close—what will be the issue? The queen gazes imploringly at Carlo, in whom the king sees the arch-contriver of the intrigue, and whom he orders to keep to his singing and not to meddle in other matters. Now follows a surprising turn— Carlo (so he himself asserts) can sing no longer, for secret distress with regard to his sister (observe, that even now the king does not know that Casilda is Carlo's sister), whom a powerful personage plans to abduct and seduce, torments him. He can divulge the name of this personage only in strictest privacy. The king promises to inflict fearful punishment on the wretch, and then hears—that he himself is the transgressor. And in connection herewith Carlo likewise reveals the inquisitor's intrigue against the queen, to prove which he has the letter from Sardinia. But Carlo, at the same time, can solemnly assure the king that he alone knows the king's secret, the queen not sharing in it. That this secret may be forever buried, he offers his own life as a sacrifice, if only Casilda be made happy with Rafael. Thereupon, Carlo and Casilda together intone their mother's song of entreaty,

and the deeply affected king solemnly vows
to remain true to the queen, to restrain the
machinations of the inquisitor, and to unite
Rafael and Casilda (an admirable disen-
tangling of the knot in a few words!). Rafael
is made a Count, and remarks that this time
he need not be anxious about the Devil's
portion; but in this, too, Carlo takes his part:
Casilda, as Rafael now learns at last (!), is not
really a she-devil, but—the sister of Carlo. So
the latter, after all, gets the best of the bargain;
he feels that Rafael and Casilda are happy,
and it is to him that they owe their happiness.

He who cannot learn the difficult art of
the successful dénouement from the masterly
construction of these scenes, can hardly hope
to master it. Follow up the manner in which
Scribe lifts the veil, bit by bit, and yet re-
serves a telling stroke for the very end.

The musical harvest shows an ampler
yield only from the beginning of the exquisitely
constructed finale (Scene 9). Before that
Carlo's solo scene, and the duet between Rafael
and Casilda, were the only "composable"
passages; still, these situations outweigh in
value a larger number. For all the various
little sleight-of-hand tricks, which attract no
special notice in the theatre, "Le Part du
Diable" is one of the very best and cleverest
librettos extant.

Admittedly, the character-drawing is its least successful feature, the distribution of light and shadow being too unequal; the queen and Carlo fairly ooze magnanimity, whereas the inquisitor is a regular stage-villain and intriguer. On the other side, Rafael and Casilda are a typical pair of lovers, drawn in the stereotyped style. As more interesting characters there remain only the vacillating king and Vargas, wavering between the parties, of whom the latter, by reason of his blending of fatuity, slyness, and malevolence, certainly offers the most grateful rôle from a histrionic standpoint. As already pointed out, Scribe was not eminent in characterization. What made him the most significant dramatic talent of the period around 1850, and possibly raises him above the dramaturgists of all times, was his knowledge of the stage, the secret of effective situations, his scenic instinct, his craftsmanship. As a living contradiction Scribe shows us how, without being properly a poet, one may nevertheless possess an immense dramatic talent. He realized the method by which, in the blaze of the footlights, routine and clever manœuvering win more numerous and sincere admirers than heartfelt and thoughtful simplicity. Scribe was for this reason, keeping in view his strong and weak points, such an admirable librettist

—one whom we certainly need not imitate, but from whom we may learn infinitely much, more particularly economy of resources.

In an opera-book elegance of language and flow of ideas are not merely superfluous, or at least not indispensable, but usually even an obstacle for the composer. Emotions and passions must be expressed in the book only in summary fashion, as it were; the situations themselves have the effect of their full dramatic impetus. The concise scenic phrase, *la parola scenica*, that Verdi always demanded in place of flowery, complicated poetry from his librettists, the word made equally manifest to the eye by a gesture, found its master in Eugène Scribe.

CONCLUSION

We have reached the end. Only suggestions could be offered, nothing more. This book is not meant to be a compendium of esthetic scholastic wisdom, but a practical manual of the handicraft. While until now I have felt obliged to sound a warning against the *under*estimation of technic, I must here no less urgently advise against its *over*estimation. Mere technic is not enough; if your work carries no message beyond that to the heart, if it lacks electrifying fancies, it may possibly win momentary plaudits, but can never possess enduring value. The goal worthy of the dramatist's striving should be the permanent inclusion of his work in the theatrical repertory. Only such works show true vital strength as maintain their places year in, year out, undiscarded.

Again, no stageplay can be completed at the writing-table; only direct contact with the living stage makes many things clear to the author. It is desirable, to begin with, that the librettist should be on such terms with the stage-management, that he may be enabled to establish the essential requirements of his work with the assistance of the regular operatic stage-director. Unfortunately, the importance of the art of stage-management (which is not identical with opulence of stage-setting) for the operatic stage is still insufficiently understood. Any new work may be irretrievably ruined by a bad performance; it is only the old, time-tested works that cannot be "ridden to death," because the audience still holds in imagination a memory of better performances, and either recognizes the poor interpretation for what it is, or unconsciously imposes its earlier and more favorable impressions on the present performance. So one should never praise a work before the evening of its première. All prophetic words may then be scattered to scorn. But, whatever the outcome, so long as the author has done his part, he knows that he did not hide his talent in the earth, that his work expresses the best that is in him, both technically and emotionally. He should not, therefore, be disheartened by temporary ill success, for all earnest endeavor is sooner or later almost certain to reap its reward. The success of "fads" and "sensations" generally dies down as swiftly as it blazed up. But a work that gains ground slowly and gradually—how long a time did Wagner's "Tristan" require!—is assured of a permanent place. In the case of many a masterpiece—we mention only Rossini's "Barber" and Bizet's "Carmen"—

it was the public, not the author that fell, short. But after-times have usually—though often enough, alas, too late—atoned for the sins of contemporaries. And a genuine artist will not allow himself to be daunted by any obstacles whatsoever.

ALLA BREVE:
From Bach *to* Debussy

By CARL ENGEL

*A*S the title suggests, these are thumb-nail sketches of the great masters of music from Bach to Debussy. We know of no book exactly like this one. The author, whose brilliant essays in The Musical Quarterly have delighted so many readers, has done his work exceedingly well, as was to be expected. The book is historical, esthetic, critical, but at the same time educational—a dangerous combination by an author of less knowledge and taste. But Mr. Engel has succeeded beyond this—he has produced a book which it is a joy to read as literature.

Price, $2.00, net

. . .

G. SCHIRMER, INC.

3 E. 43rd St.   New York

A 645

WS - #0042 - 071020 - C0 - 229/152/10 - PB - 9781334045615